3230244882
Library
WITHDRAWN

The Essential Guide

Greta McGough

CARDONALD COLLEGE LRC
362 MCG 32302
8292 44882

Domestic Violence – The Essential Guide is also available in accessible formats for people with any degree of visual impairment. The large print edition and eBook (with accessibility features enabled) are available from Need2Know. Please let us know if there are any special features you require and we will do our best to accommodate your needs.

First published in Great Britain in 2011 by
Need2Know
Remus House
Coltsfoot Drive
Peterborough
PE2 9JX
Telephone 01733 898103
Fax 01733 313524
www.need2knowbooks.co.uk

All Rights Reserved
© Greta McGough 2011
SB ISBN 978-1-86144-223-9
Cover photograph: Dreamstime

Contents

Introduction

Unfortunately, domestic violence remains a fact of life for far too many people. Well over 90% of these are women. There are instances of males being abused by their female partners, but in fact a different psychology appears to be in place, and it's important to keep sight of the main facts and scenarios. Because domestic violence by far and away targets women in number, I will usually use the female pronoun throughout this book when referring to victims. Male nouns and pronouns will be used, but mostly when referring to abusers and perpetrators of violence. This is a reflection of the overwhelming figures, so no sexism intended.

Within this book, you will find a wide-ranging guide to the problems (and its results) which will be of use to individuals, families, friends and health professionals everywhere. Pseudonyms are used and indicated with an asterix*.

If you are (or someone you know is) suffering from domestic violence, this book will help you to deal with problems, and begin to rebuild your life.

Exercise

The statistics tell us that one in four women is (or has been) abused by a partner in our society. So, if not you, then someone you know. You may want to pause for a moment and consider that. Include in your thoughts family members, especially the older ones, and allow yourself to wonder. Can you recall any unusual circumstances that a woman you know offered explanations for, but which really did not add up?

Can you recall how you responded?

Did you assume that she 'would tell me if she wanted to'? Did you decide not to embarrass her by asking further questions? Don't worry if you did. We are all human, and this is difficult!

Women in trouble

Pause now, to consider the questions in the box on the previous page, before reading on. You will find a scenario to consider in each of the chapters. None of them are easy questions to answer, and are certainly not designed to make you feel you have failed a friend! But they will help you to learn, and to gain the necessary concepts.

A woman in trouble suffers from more than bruises and broken bones. What actually happens in a domestic violence scenario, is usually more than physical violence, and will be discussed in later chapters. It is important to understand these other factors in the event, so that we can see what is really happening to the woman, and how terribly she may be scarred in unseen, emotional ways.

What is important is that (whether professional or layperson) you begin to realise that you can be of help to others, sometimes just by listening, when a victim comes to the day that she can no longer keep silent about her situation.

'A woman in trouble suffers from more than bruises and broken bones.'

Several of these chapters focus upon regaining mental and physical health, self-esteem and returning to a fuller and happier life.

It is easy not to spot the signs, even the obvious ones, and to assume that everything is wonderful, when someone we care about might well be suffering in silence. A friend (professional or otherwise) who can help an abused woman to talk, is taking a big step towards helping her to regain her freedom, her health and possibly even her life. (Iwi, Newman; 2011)

Families

It is easy to feel embarrassed by the possibility that domestic violence is occurring, and to feel that if we ask or enquire, our friend may see it as intrusive. Even health professionals such as nurses are often unsure of their ground, and an opportunity to help someone may be lost. (Bradbury-Jones, 2011; Trevillon K et al, 2011). The victim may become angry or distressed, and we may lose her friendship. But there are ways to allow individuals space, so that they come to a day when they can talk. The road towards this point is a subtle one, and we must tread carefully – but firmly. My intention here is to give ordinary women (both the abused and their friends or family, as well as professionals) the courage to approach the issues.

I have included a list of some of the organisations that can help, in cases of domestic violence. Don't assume that nothing has changed in the last decades. There is more help available out there than you might think.

A word to professionals

Health professionals need to know how domestic violence may be the underlying cause of whatever the patient has presented with. Within the professional role, it is possible to look at the woman holistically (that is, the whole person) and to allow space for a wider discussion of the issues, as the woman herself feels she can confide.

'It takes a lot of courage for someone to tell you their "dreadful dark secret".'

References are included at the back of the book, should you wish to read further. I have included the ones that worked for me in the writing of this book.

It takes several weeks (maybe longer) before an abused woman will allow herself to trust a professional, however kind they may be to her. About six weeks into a counselling situation, on average, the truth may begin to be tentatively explored – by the client. Then it is important not to miss the cues and clues that will allow that person the space to talk safely.

Our responses, when someone begins to confide, are vital. We should never respond judgementally or negatively. Remember that it takes a lot of courage for someone to tell you their 'dreadful dark secret'. Chapter 3 'Talking to Someone' will allow us to look at situations, and to practice responses that make for good listening skills. As professionals, good listening skills are essential to our good practise, and we should never let them slip, or become casual about them. It is not an exaggeration to say that you might be saving someone's life.

I have not touched upon abuse of children or elder abuse in this book, since both of these are massive problems in their own right. Instead I have concentrated upon the traditional scenario, where a (controlling) male figure beats and intimidates a (cowed and now submissive) female partner.

Disclaimer

The results of domestic violence are far-ranging, and cause considerable further serious issues, within health care. (Trevillon K et al, 2011). We may not feel comfortable addressing this problem, but if we do, we will be able to help an individual back to a fuller, healthier and happier life. This book will allow us all to feel more confident about addressing the issues, professional or layperson alike. However, this book is meant as a general guide, not a replacement for professional help and counselling.

Chapter One

Definitions

While violence of any kind is fairly self-explanatory, domestic violence contains certain key features. Pause for a moment, and write notes describing what you would expect to find. Think of the people involved and use words to describe them. You may have some very firm ideas about what is happening and what has led people there. It is possible that as you read this book, some of these will be adjusted or developed, so keep your list and return to it later. The rest of this chapter contains some thoughts on what domestic violence is.

History

'There have always been those who imposed their will upon others.'

Domestic violence is as old as human society. There have always been those who imposed their will upon others who were physically less strong, and used both their fists and cruel words to enforce their will. Why some people do this will be discussed later – but understanding motivation is never any help to the victim. She (almost immediately) becomes concerned only with ways to survive, and makes rapid adjustments to her view of the world in an attempt to make sense of it all.

A victim's individual history is not a real guide to what is going on. There are many (misleading) misconceptions about why a woman finds herself in this position, and these are largely expressed by people who have never woken up one day to find that it has happened. There is no doubt that if – as a child – you witnessed domestic violence in the family, you will more readily accept this as the norm. This is a powerful argument for leaving the situation when you have children, so that abuse does not continue for another generation. (Jaffe et al, 2011)

Control

Perhaps the key issue above all others is that of control – one person feels an overwhelming need to control the lives of those people nearest and dearest to him. While physical violence may stop for periods of time, emotional violence doesn't. Women describe the impossibility of going to the shops and missing the bus home, since their partner will assume that she is doing something he disapproves of. Violence will follow. Access to money is kept to a minimum, since abusers can see that a woman with any money of her own may one day find a way to leave.

The other side of the control issue, then is the victim's own lack of control over her life. The abuser takes away her rights and support as well as her access to money, and she quickly loses belief in herself as a person. All domestic violence is accompanied by the repeated statement that she has done something to deserve this. The victim will try to agree with her abuser, so as not to incur his anger, but in fact this only puts her instantly and emotionally on the wrong foot. It is much easier to fall into this trap than to climb out of it. Human beings have emotional needs, and try to fit in with their circumstances in order to achieve them. We easily believe the worst of ourselves if someone makes cruel remarks. We can readily accept another's (inaccurate) description of ourselves, because of the fears we all carry inside. (Abrahams H, 2010)

'The abuser takes away her rights and support as well as her access to money, and she quickly loses belief in herself as a person.'

Facts and figures

The facts and figures state that one in four women in the Western world suffer from domestic violence at some time. If you're not a victim yourself, or don't work amongst women who have been emotionally damaged, you may find this hard to believe. However, if you are (or have been) a victim you will find the telltale signs much easier to spot, and it may be that the figure appears higher. (Mann, Cunningham, 2009)

How accurate can figures on domestic violence ever be? By its nature, domestic violence is a secretive thing. Victims are ashamed of the situation, which, remember, their abuser has repeatedly told them they deserve. Intelligent women can very easily find themselves locked into this nightmare emotional trap. They are ashamed to let anyone know that their private life is such a disaster, and that they don't know how to escape. When women do manage to escape, they have often not involved the police or any support organisation, from which figures are drawn.

It seems likely then, that the figures are not accurate – that in fact they may be much higher. We can never really know. One thing is certain, however. If a proportion of men have the habit of physically abusing their women, the majority do not. Those inclined to abuse share characteristics, and someone who – for no definite reason – reminds you of your ex may well think as he did, and should be avoided. These are important facts to remember, when a victim is trying to put her life back together.

Behind closed doors

Domestic violence is a very secret affair. One characteristic that most abusers share is to keep that secret, and to force their victim to keep it. The threat is more – worse – violence, and often threat of death. An abuser will repeatedly remind a victim that he is capable of killing both her and her children if she even speaks about the situation to anyone.

'With hindsight, it is possible to look back and see telltale signs.'

A person's home should be the place they are able to to feel safe in. For victims of violence it is not. Hannah* says that, 'After I left, I felt as though a weight had been lifted. I was always afraid at home, always making sure that the doors and windows were locked. When I got away, that fear left me, and I realised that what I feared was inside the house, not a threat from outside. I had been trying to lock doors against the man who was already inside my home.'

How quickly things change

While a woman may be aware that her partner 'has a temper', it is a shock when she finds that she may become the focus of it. The first physical violence is always a shock. With hindsight, it is possible to look back and see telltale signs, such as an insistence upon things his own way, a certain obsessionalism, a tendency to drink too much and become angry. But no one ever thinks they will become the focus of his anger. Once you stay, it is hard to leave, because his words have already sunk into your subconscious. But it is hard to walk away after the first attack. No one ever believes that it will happen again.

If this has been your experience, don't think of yourself as foolish. You are only human, and we humans always want to believe that our lives will work out. To find yourself in the trap doesn't mean you lack intelligence. But surviving and trying to make sense of the world are now priority. Knowing that you are intelligent can make you feel more guilty and ashamed for letting it happen. You are not. We'll return to this later, when we look at how to return to normal life.

Secrets and lies

All types of abuse involve – as part of the enforcement of control – the abuser insisting that the victim keeps abuse a secret. Abusers lie to disguise the situation or to confuse any ideas that outsiders might get about what is going on. The main way of enforcing this is to threaten the victim with even greater violence should she tell anyone else what is happening. (Neale, 2011)

'The secrets and lies that a victim is forced into are damaging in themselves.'

The victim is therefore forced to lie about her injuries. Concealing them may not be enough. They may be noticed by a friend or a professional, and questioned. Famously we claim to have 'walked into a cupboard door' and so on.

The secrets and lies that a victim is forced into are damaging in themselves. When someone is forced to live within this web of secrecy, they quickly begin to lose all sense of their identity and certainty (apart from fear) in the world they live in. Secrets and lies are a huge part of the de-humanising process, and a main part of the abuser's control.

Professionals beginning to gain someone's trust may be asked by the victim 'not to say anything'. The correct professional response to this is to say that they must document what is said, but can respect the victim's wish that it is not disclosed at this time. That request should be documented, too. If the day comes that the abused person needs legal help, an official record is an important item.

A professional is also a human being, and it is legitimate to say to the victim, 'This is something I've no experience with, but I'd like to discuss it with my colleague, so that together we can find ways to help you.' A victim may retreat at this point from further disclosure, but the conversation must be documented. It is vital that the client knows her wishes are respected, and that the door is open if she wishes to discuss things further.

Anyone who has secrets and lies imposed upon them is a victim. The best way to deal with this is to speak to someone, despite the threats that have been made. Disclosure will be treated as you wish and voicing what is happening will go a long way to realising that there is a life beyond your situation.

Depression and suicide

Living in a violent world has many more effects than damaging your body and making you feel worthless. Real clinical depression is likely to develop and the world becomes an ever-increasing trap. When we hear someone say that they feel trapped, alarm bells should ring. They are telling us that they feel they have run out of options in life, and that their perspective is no longer one where they can make reasonable decisions. The statement 'I feel trapped' is usually offered in a quiet way, which might be mistaken for something that is not very important. It could therefore be dismissed, mistaken or ignored. However, it is an important statement. This is usually the point where the victim is beginning to explore her nightmare, and to voice things at all is progress. She is also (whether she realises it or not) checking out the person she has chosen to speak to. If that person reacts carelessly or does not give her feelings weight, the moment may be lost, and she may not speak again. She may move on instead to considering a more permanent way out of her trap.

'When we hear someone say that they feel trapped, alarm bells should ring.'

For many victims, thoughts of suicide rear their heads and can seem to be 'the only way out'. Of course it is not, but once ideas of suicide begin to take hold, they quickly become a part of life and are very difficult to dislodge. Anyone expressing suicidal thoughts should be taken seriously and the assumption should never be made that 'people who talk about it never do it'. Women with children who actually attempt suicide may also decide that their children would be better off dead, too. It is not unknown for a woman to attempt suicide after killing her children, but to survive herself.

If someone expresses suicidal thoughts to you, help must be sought. An individual feeling suicidal can always phone the Samaritans, and will find someone to help them at the end of the line. Women's Aid, who provide the refuges, are a good source of help and also provide 'drop-in' facilities in many places, at certain times. The local emergency mental health team can also be contacted by phone. There is a phone number for them in every area of the country.

Don't assume that someone already needs to be known to the system for the emergency mental health team to respond to them. The person telephoning should be able to explain the situation fully and should know a few basic facts, such as age and perhaps the name of the GP. They should also be able to wait with the sufferer until the team arrive, because there may well be a delay in their arrival.

There are no magic wands. Simply expressing pent-up feelings does not make the urge to commit suicide disappear, but it is a vital first step on the road to survival. Be sure – if someone shares their desperate feelings with you – that you do not walk away without listening, and close the door that has been so hard for them to open.

Safety

There are safe places in the world, but these are hard to see when you are the victim of domestic violence. The Women's Aid Federation provides helplines and supplies temporary refuges as well as drop-in centres in some places. There are never going to be enough of these. But that should not stop us from making contact with those who can listen to us and provide help and support as we begin to move forward.

'In the world of domestic violence, there is no sense of safety.'

Many women dislike the idea of the refuge, even when they are desperate. They assume the worst when they imagine it. They are invariably pleasantly surprised. It is important to realise that there may simply be no space available when you need the refuge, but that those volunteers working the helpline will still be able to offer support, and a drop-in centre may provide an hour or two of respite every week.

In the world of domestic violence, there is no sense of safety. A safe place might be found, but the first casualty of domestic violence is the victim's sense of trust and security. Unfortunately, many victims who succeed in escaping the situation struggle to regain their sense of safety, even after many years. The habit of looking over the shoulder remains. However good life becomes after escape, the worry that the abuser may reappear persists.

We will discuss safety, again, in more detail later in the book, but it is important to know that the sense of safety can be regained, even though it takes a long time.

Scenario

Jane* is a woman whose life appears to be going well. She is a qualified nurse and has recently been promoted. When her boyfriend asks her to marry him, it seems that her life will be complete.

On their honeymoon, he has been drunk for three days, when she tells him it is time to sober up, so that they can share the sort of honeymoon she has always dreamed of. His violence is startling and terrifying. Nothing in her life has ever prepared her for this. Half an hour later, she finds herself alone in the room, bruised and bleeding and completely confused about the new side of him that she has seen.

What should she do? He has her passport and the tickets, and she has no money to go home. How can she go back to her family and friends, and admit that her marriage is a terrible mistake? Surely his drinking is only because he is on holiday, and it has just got out of hand? Surely this can only be a one-off? He has never shown this capacity for violence before.

This is not how she sees herself. But he told her again and again as he was beating her, that she had no right to question him. She must be more careful in the future.

She always said that she would never put up with something like this. But she cannot bring herself to tell anyone what has happened and decides to give him another chance.

Will she find it easier or harder to leave, when it happens again?

Summing Up

- Anyone finding themselves in a world that is suddenly defined by domestic violence immediately loses certain key factors in life. These include their sense of worth, their ability to trust and to feel secure and their belief in themselves as masters of their own fate. These losses mean that the bottom literally falls out of their world, and they are in the deep 'black hole' that is so difficult to climb out of.
- This experience is a common one. If it does not apply to you, it is certainly happening (or has happened) to someone you know. Do not make the mistake of believing that victims choose (or even enjoy!) this way of life, or that they are stupid and inclined to perpetuate the situation. To voice these mistaken ideas is to collude with the abuser, whose power lies in the promotion of his victim in this way.
- To help to fight the abuser's cruelty, try to find ways to help the abused to regain a sense of self-worth, and allow her to know that she can find a way forward. She will begin to find that way forward by first finding someone who will listen, and who might help her find a space to explore the possibilities that suit her.

'Do not make the mistake of believing that victims choose (or even enjoy!) this way of life.'

Chapter Two

Relationships

The abusive relationship is, by definition, unequal and the abuser puts a lot of time and energy into keeping it that way. An abusive relationship is a powerful thing and it would be wrong of us to think of control and terror as any less powerful than love. Because human beings very easily take on board negative views of themselves, the trap that is the basis of an abusive relationship is very difficult to escape from.

Other relationships suffer. The abuser makes the effort to separate the victim from anyone who might be sympathetic to her or provide her with a listening ear. Family and friends who genuinely care about the victim are rapidly excluded from life – and any contact with them provides the abuser with an excuse for further violence. If you find yourself excluded from someone's life after they become involved with a particular person, it is easy at first to assume that this is normal and that they have simply taken another direction. Or you might take offence and 'leave them to it'. It is not so easy to recognise that your friend may actually be very afraid of their partner, and that contact from you and others will cause them to suffer both physically and emotionally. (O'Shea 2011)

'The abuser makes the effort to separate the victim from anyone who might be sympathetic.'

People do sometimes change towards their family and friends when they become involved with a new partner, without violence being involved. You may find that you instinctively do not like your friend's partner and assume that he feels the same about you. This may be (on the surface at least) reason enough to lose the friendship. If, however, all other family and friends are being excluded from their life, there may well be something more sinister going on. Even so, you cannot easily find a way to break through the walls that he is building.

If you can let your friend know that, whatever happens, you will always be there if she decides to confide her troubles to you, that may help her at a later date, even if it is months or even years later. But she may never be able to do this. She may well believe that any such discussion would mean that she is disloyal and therefore deserves the fury and abuse that outside contact will create. There is no way that someone can break through this from outside. Psychologically, the victim is already caught in the beliefs that her abuser has enforced upon her.

Perhaps you can find a way to 'accidentally' see your friend, but you will find (if she is in trouble) that her partner does not allow her to deviate from the set routine of the day, by stopping to chat or for coffee. Sometimes the best you can do is to remind her of good times you had, so that one day when she is desperate for someone to talk to, she may think of you.

'The victim appears to change and her lack of confidence becomes evident.'

Warning signs

These changes in a person's attitude to her family and friends are the first of the warning signs that appear to the outside world. The victim appears to change and her lack of confidence becomes evident. She is more nervous about things that never used to trouble her. She may make jokes that involve the mention of violence, which she previously would not have thought funny. This is because violence has become a part of her life.

Victims of domestic violence classically show a lack of interest in activities that used to be enjoyed. This is known as 'anhedonia' (emotional deadness),and includes distancing oneself from people, and/or not being able to think about the future or make future plans. Victims often suggest that they believe they might not live much longer. They seem to stop worrying about this possibility and accept the idea of a shortened lifespan stoically.

Victims may also suffer from a generalised anxiety disorder (GAD). This is a condition which is characterised by six months or more of chronic, exaggerated worry and tension – and which is unfounded or much more severe than the normal anxiety most people experience. Sufferers always expect the worst in life. They worry excessively about everything – money, health, family or work, even when there are no outward signs of trouble. They struggle to relax and often suffer from insomnia. Sometimes the source of the worry is hard to pinpoint. Simply the thought of getting through the day provokes anxiety. Many sufferers also have physical symptoms, such as fatigue, trembling, muscle tension, headaches, irritability or hot flashes. They may feel lightheaded or out of breath. They also may feel queasy or have to go to the bathroom frequently.

Some of these 'nervous' symptoms also form part of a condition known as 'Hyperarousal', which stems from high levels of anxiety. In addition to problems falling or staying asleep, sufferers feel more irritable and are prone to outbursts of anger. They have difficulty concentrating. They feel 'jumpy' or easily startled. They feel that danger may be lurking around every corner and that they must be constantly 'on guard'.

If you suffer from these warning signs, or you observe them in someone else, then help is needed – whether physical violence is part of the picture or not. However, the abuser will do everything he can to stop help being received and, to muddy the waters, when descriptions of symptoms are taken. The warning signs that a person may be an abuser include being discovered in this sort of sabotage. Many abusers are very convincing in their explanations of what is happening, even to the point where the victim – as well as her family and friends – begin to doubt the truth of their own experience or observations.

'An abuser is rarely at a loss for an explanation.'

An abuser is rarely at a loss for an explanation, whereas, someone with nothing to hide is uncertain about events at some time in their lives. Abusers never are. They have their explanations and answers ready. They are usually ahead of everyone else in order to maintain life as they want it to be. In this they are very manipulative.

An abuser (or potential abuser) will often betray their basic nature by displaying a talent for mental cruelty long before they become physical. They have a talent for knowing other people's weak spots and exploiting them. If someone has an uncertainty in their life, the abuser will, at some point, 'push the buttons' to make them feel anxious or guilty, simply because they can. Such a person may be seen as attempting to cover up their own uncertainties, but this is no excuse for exceeding basic human boundaries. What they are doing (habitually) is a measure of their need for control and to manipulate any situation.

When we begin a relationship with someone new, if we find that they operate in this way it is best to leave. This may sound easy to say and difficult to do, but the future is bleak the longer we stay with that person. It is important to remember that normal human beings do not operate in this way and that you deserve a life where you are not made to feel bad.

All abusers tell victims that they deserve the treatment they are getting. It is very easy for victims to believe this and to believe that they have caused the abuse. They quickly believe that they are a person who 'attracts a certain type' – which is another way of saying that the fault lies in the victim. Family and friends who agree with this are putting final nails into the coffin.

Warning signs are plain, but we often don't want to see them. We can bury our heads in the sand and accept life as dictated by the abuser, or we can argue against accepting the world as he wants it to be. His need for control is not to be encouraged or supported. (Griffiths, 2011)

'All abusers tell victims that they deserve the treatment they are getting.'

Control

The abuser's need to control others is at the heart of so much that happens. The question 'why does he do that?' (Bancroft, 2003) has often been asked, and the abuser's own inadequacies and insecurities, personal history and so on, are often cited. However, he is unlikely to change. Factors such as alcohol and drug abuse play a large part in domestic violence, but again individuals can only move away from addiction because they want to, not to please or accommodate anyone else and their needs.

We return to the issue of control again and again throughout this book. One person aims to control another. A key part of the strategy is to take away any sense that the victim has of control over her own life or fate. She must be kept in a constant state of uncertainty for his controlling tactics to work. This includes being kept constantly without a sense of personal control.

Once certainty is lost in life, we struggle to move forward or to make sense of life. That is not to say that control of our lives can't be regained, but it is a hard struggle and may well take years to achieve. Because something is difficult – and looks impossible from certain angles – doesn't mean we should give up. It can be done. We will look at ways forward later in the book, both from the point of view of the victim and those who care for them. When we look at ways back to personal self-esteem, one of the key issues is to practise believing that control over life can be achieved. This is a huge step for victims, but when we begin to take steps back towards normal life, we must do it by building on basics such as this.

Agoraphobia

You may know of agoraphobia as a fear of open spaces, but it may also include general social anxiety. The result of this is that a sufferer will leave the house less and less and will reduce their interaction with others drastically.

When a person begins to act increasingly in this way, help is needed. Professionals may become involved at this point. This may be the GP or the community mental health team. What is interesting is that the abuser may well appear to allow this to happen. He may present to the world as a very caring individual, who wishes his partner to recover, but this may be a cover-up for subtle sabotage of her efforts. The gain he makes from allowing this scenario to develop is that the victim now has a label: 'history of mental illness', which he may use at a later date to rubbish any claims she becomes brave enough to make, which show him in an abusive light. He never has any intention of allowing her to regain mental health, since her confusion and fear – now projected away from him and on to the outside world – serve him well in his need for control.

'He may present to the world as a very caring individual, who wishes his partner to recover.'

Health professionals should observe the partners of agoraphobic sufferers for telltale signs that they are in fact sabotaging the sufferer's progress, treatment, sense of self-worth and ability to communicate. The abuser at this point will be at his most charming and appear extremely concerned and caring.

In acute stress disorder, symptoms persist from two days to four weeks, rather than the long-term existence of agoraphobia. But it is important to recognise that anxiety states all have their root somewhere and that sufferers often find it difficult to admit (even to themselves) what the real cause may be. Long term, we begin to see the symptoms of post-traumatic stress, which we will give a chapter to later on. But all these conditions edge on to each other, are worthy of professional attention and probably share the same cause. Other symptoms include problems regulating feelings. This may result in suicidal thoughts or explosive anger. Victims may show a tendency to forget the trauma or say that they feel detached from life (dissociation) or body (depersonalisation). They describe persistent feelings of helplessness, shame, guilt, or of 'being completely different' from others. They may come to believe that the abuser is all-powerful and may become preoccupied with ideas of revenge.

Symbiosis

The word symbiosis describes a way in which two organisms function in relation to each other. This word originates in sciences that deal with plants or animals, but you may also hear the phrase 'symbiotic relationship' used sometimes in human psychology. The definition tells us that in some symbiotic relationships both symbionts entirely depend on each other for survival. In other relationships they can, but do not have to, live with the other organism.

'The abuser has usually created a situation that has made the victim totally emotionally dependent upon him.'

Symbiotic relationships include those associations in which one organism lives on another or where one partner lives inside the other. What does this mean when the phrase is used in the context of human beings? Two human beings appear to become interdependent, but do not particularly appear to care for each other. Yet the status quo between them and the habits that define their existence are very pronounced. As people sometimes say – 'can't live with 'em, can't live without 'em'.

In domestic violence, the abuser has usually created a situation that has made the victim totally emotionally dependent upon him. He has removed links to outside family, friends and work situations. The victim's dependence is fairly obvious and she is no longer allowed to express opinions or to express her feelings and emotions, because this will make her abuser feel threatened and angry. Women describe this in different ways. Margaret*, an accomplished artist, found herself forbidden not only to paint, but even to pick up a pencil and doodle. This was as cruel an imposition upon her as her abuser could devise, since it denied her basic nature. If she spoke out of turn, expressed an opinion or was discovered having sketched something, the violence that followed was terrible.

It is worth remembering that when you begin to progress back towards a sense of 'self', aspects of your personality such as this are often key to health and survival. When Margaret* left her husband to live alone, she covered her walls with sketches and drawings. She described how these helped her to rediscover herself. There is no doubt that within every victim there are things that help them to define themselves. Sometimes abuse and the habit of confinement make victims even forget what these are, but they are there. We will return to this later in the book, when we look at ways to rediscover ourselves.

The abuser in a symbiotic relationship is dependent on his victim in a less obvious way. Because he keeps control of everything in their life, dependence may not be a word that springs to mind when we look at him. However, his need for control can be thought of as a kind of addiction. He needs his victim to be under his control. Victims report again and again that any moment where he fears they will step out of the lines he has drawn causes a fury in him that results in extreme mental and physical cruelty.

Jackie* described a favourite CD whose music reminded her of happy times before she was married, and which she played to herself after being beaten, to calm her shattered nerves. Her husband's response on discovering this was to destroy the CD and to forbid her to play any music.

'His need for control can be thought of as a kind of addiction.'

She left him later, but the power of his 'rules' had become so deeply embedded in her mind that it was several years before she felt she could allow herself to play that music. Again, when we begin to look for factors that will help to heal us and recover, a favourite piece of music can be a powerful thing. When the time comes that a victim feels she can move on in life, it is important to cultivate a sense of defiance, and to consciously choose to do things that have been forbidden for so long.

Finally, money. The abuser keeps control by also keeping control of any money that the victim has or earns. He needs her money and quickly becomes dependent himself upon that money. He has taken this as his right for so long, that he can no longer see why she should not provide added income for his needs.

Stella* recalls the day that she let slip that she was leaving. She feared a violent outburst as a result of this, but was determined this time that she would not back down and that she would carry out her plan. Perhaps he saw a change in her, a new determination and realised that his tactics would no longer work. 'His eyes filled with tears,' she said. 'I said to him "no emotional blackmail, Jack*, I'm not listening". And he turned round and said to me, "You can't do this to me, Stella*. I can't live without your salary." Liberating words. I wish he'd said that years ago! I'd always fallen for the line that he needed me, and mistaken that for love. Now I knew that I'd never been anything to him but a meal ticket. It was easy to leave after that.'

All of which goes to show, even the constraints of a long-established symbiotic relationship can be broken. The first step is for the victim to recognise that she has a right to her own life. We will look at what follows this first step later, in more detail.

Alcohol

'Partners may expect and demand that we drink (or do drugs) with them so our own judgement becomes clouded.'

Alcoholism (also known as alcohol dependence) and other addictions are huge factors in domestic abuse. Because excessive use of any substance is part of the way of life and does not become excessive overnight, it is sometimes difficult to realise that use has passed normal boundaries and become excessive. Partners may expect and demand that we drink (or do drugs) with them so our own judgement becomes clouded and we may be in danger of developing a problem of our own. Saying 'no' to the demands of an angry, violent partner who wants you to drink with him, is extremely difficult. It is all too easy to accept the numbing effects of alcohol, which seem to give some respite from the pain, terror and constant uncertainty that have come to characterise life.

Some women find that refusing alcohol simply does not work. Their refusal always results in a violent attack. They then find ways of pretending to drink, while repeatedly getting rid of the alcohol that their partner insists they should take. Their partner goes through the stages of alcohol use, finally passing out. At this point he can be covered with a quilt and left to sleep it off. Liz* described sometimes managing to pour herself a glass of water, which she then drank in place of the vodka that her husband insisted on. She was afraid at first that he would realise there was no smell of alcohol on her breath, but of course he tasted and smelt alcohol from his own intake, so this was never an issue.

Because of its nature, excessive use of alcohol within a partnership may have crept up and gone unrecognised for a long, long time. There are many ways in which excessive alcohol use affects different people. (Harrington-Lowe 2008). Some are binge drinkers but some drink steadily, constantly 'topping up' their blood alcohol levels. What is certain is that excessive use of alcohol causes great changes in a person's life. They fail to operate to the best of their potential. They struggle to maintain relationships, since their main priority is drink, rather than another person, or even regard for themselves.

Alcoholism is characterised by four basic symptoms: craving, tolerance, loss of control and physical dependence.

Alcoholism is a disease. Alcoholism is chronic; it lasts a lifetime. Of course it is not infectious, but living close to an alcoholic (spouse, parent, etc.) can cause us to adopt the way of life and develop certain attitudes to drink. The craving for alcohol can be as strong as the need for food or water. Alcoholics continue to drink, despite serious family, health or legal problems.

Alcoholism cannot be cured. There is never a day when it is safe for an alcoholic to drink again. Not drinking is the only safe course for most people with alcoholism. But it can be treated. Alcoholism treatment programmes use both counselling and medications to help a person stop drinking. Treatment has helped many people stop drinking and rebuild their lives. Those who are successful over long periods of time are those who become involved with Alcoholics Anonymous and draw support from them.

'There is never a day when it is safe for an alcoholic to drink again.'

The alcoholic must wish to change their life – enough to want to stop drinking. This is not something that another person can persuade someone to do, or impose upon them. Only a personal decision to change can be the basis for recovery, and for a return to health and normal relationships.

There is help and support for the families and partners of alcoholics. While alcoholics can attend AA (Alcoholics Anonymous) meetings everywhere in Britain and in thousands of places around the world, there are also groups such as Al-Anon for partners and spouses, and Alateen for the children of alcoholics. These are less common, but can be found in all major cities. There is a great deal of honesty and support within these groups and they are recommended.

However, there may come a day when the alcoholic's need to drink is again overwhelming. As Sharon* described it, 'Suddenly someone, a stranger, looks out of his eyes. Then I know that whatever I say or do, it is going to be wrong, and he's going to batter me. Then he'll be off on a binge.' At this point, he will also forbid you to go to your support group. While the groups are anonymous, you may have established a friendship with someone from the group who can still be contacted, while you stay away for a while. Relationships such as these can be lifesavers.

Sara* was shocked when her ex-boyfriend suddenly attacked her and beat her. 'We were not a couple anymore, but I thought we were best mates . . . Yes, he was drunk, but I've never seen him like that. There was no reasoning with him. I didn't provoke him. I just didn't recognise him.'

What did Sara* do? She went to the police and filed a complaint, despite his family and friends trying to persuade her 'not to cause trouble'. Her complaint was upheld and went to court.

She still thinks it was the best thing she could have done, and would advise anyone in the same situation not to be afraid of the police. 'After all,' she says 'he would only do it again, to someone else . . . '

Scenario

Joanne* and Nick* have been together for over six years. She knows that his drinking has increased, but says that this is because of the problems that are happening at work. He is under a lot of stress. She has tried getting him to talk, but he only becomes angry. Now she wonders if she ever knew him at all.

One night, he comes home late and very drunk. She is out of her mind with worry and decides to tell him how desperate his behaviour is making her feel. He becomes abusive and hits her in the face. While she is on the floor he kicks her repeatedly with his boots. Then he goes out again.

When he returns, he says that he is very, very sorry and tells her that it will never happen again.

Should she take him at his word? Is trusting him on this the best way of showing her love and support?

Is there anyone she could ask for advice?

'I didn't provoke him. I just didn't recognise him.'

Sara*

Summing Up

- Relationships are complicated. There is never a single, simple, straightforward answer to a relationship problem. Men and women differ in their approach to problems and how to solve them. Women tend to try to talk, but many men are afraid of discussion and see the questions posed by their women as merely critical.
- Sadly, solutions can only be found if they are talked about honestly, without simply blaming and scoring points. If one (or both) parties do not want to look at the issues together, nothing can improve and trying to discuss them may even make things worse. It may well be that, finally, the relationship cannot be saved and it is best to draw a line under it and move on.
- But talking to someone – either as a couple or individually – remains the basis for change. In the next chapter we will look at some of the factors that we must consider before we open our hearts to someone else.

'Solutions can only be found if they are talked about honestly, without simply blaming and scoring points.'

Chapter Three

Talking to Someone

Fear

We may be afraid to talk to someone honestly about our lives for many reasons. The threat of more violence has already been mentioned, and this is probably the most powerful reason to remain silent. But in a violent situation, fear quickly becomes a part of everyday life and colours everything that we think and do. Opportunities to speak are limited by the threats of the abuser and so, even if someone appears who might be spoken to, it may be that this person cannot easily be contacted again.

The other two main fears that a victim has are a fear of being disbelieved and fears or worries that their own judgement and perception has become corrupted.

Victims of violence are repeatedly told that their perception is inaccurate. They are 'mad' and what they know has happened to them never did. If there is physical evidence, they are told that it did not happen how they believe it did. Their abuser often insists that what the victim remembers is inaccurate and their memory and judgement cannot be trusted. They want outsiders to believe this of the victim too.

'Victims of violence are repeatedly told that their perception is inaccurate.'

To those who have never suffered in this way, it may seem strange that anyone's self-belief can be so thoroughly undermined. And yet self-belief is a very easy thing to destroy. Physical problems, such as blows to the head, also cause mild or moderate concussion, especially if the blows fall in the 'hidden' area above the hairline. Many abusers aim for this area, because the bruising will not be visible. This leaves the victim walking around (and without facial bruising) but having to put all their energy into coping and feeling very 'cloudy' about what has led them there. To be told by a tireless abuser that their memory is faulty, is an overwhelming and powerful thing.

Fear is the main weapon that abusers use to stop victims speaking to someone and from taking the first step towards help. They take away trust in self and others, leaving them increasingly trapped, unable to take the first step towards escape.

Trust

Having lost trust in herself and others, a victim may spend months or even years in an uncertain emotional place. The first step back towards help, health and escape is to be able to trust someone enough to speak to them. This is not going to happen overnight and the abuser will work hard at keeping the victim isolated from any relationship that might support her. The fears outlined in the last section will prevent her from trusting anyone, or even her own judgement.

The victim may be afraid that someone who looks like they might be trusted may laugh at her fears and nightmare. How can the victim tell if someone is alright to talk to? Once she has escaped of course, certain professionals can be approached who will listen to her, but long before she can find the courage and strength to think about escape, she needs to have found ways to trust another human being. Plainly, this is a vicious circle that helps to keep her trapped within the violent situation.

'Trust cannot be turned on and off like a tap.'

How to trust someone or, persuading someone to trust you – is key to the way forward. It is a step that must be taken at some time, but it may be the hardest step of all. Trust cannot be turned on and off like a tap. It will take some time before someone can be trusted. They must 'prove' themselves to the victim first.

Listening skills

Professionals reading this book will already know something about the listening skills that are essential to good practice. Often, the best thing we can do for anyone is to listen (genuinely) to them. When the issue is psychological – as many of the effects of violence are – recovery is something that takes place because the sufferer is allowed to find a space where healing can happen. There are treatments, to be discussed shortly, but healing comes from within.

Physical problems arising from violence may need actual physical treatment, but for many years now, research has shown that physical healing is helped if sufferers feel that someone communicates with them. The primary factor in communication is listening, rather than giving advice.

Within listening skills, there are several key factors:

- Remaining silent; allowing the victim to speak at her own pace and in her own way.
- Not making assumptions about situations or what is being disclosed.
- Not giving advice. Some professionals – and many friends – find this hard to do. Sometimes victims ask for advice and it becomes difficult to avoid. However, the best response is to encourage someone to make their own choices and decisions. Whenever we do this, we are fostering the regrowth of selfesteem and self-reliance – both of which have been damaged or destroyed by the climate of violence.
- Never rushing the victim. Talking takes time, and it is important that she proceeds at her own pace and in her own way.
- Reflecting back what has been said in a gentle, non-judgemental way, at regular intervals. In this, the victim makes a statement and the listener reflects the words back as a question. This makes sure that there is no misunderstanding and also allows the victim to know that she is being fully listened to, which will encourage her to speak a little more.

'Talking takes time.'

There is no substitute for this type of professional approach. To stray from these rules as a listener is to undermine the foundations that the victim needs to build, to redevelop trust and overcome fear.

Types of therapy

During therapy, a sufferer talks to a trained mental health-care professional who helps her to identify and work through the issues. A victim may find herself needing therapy either after escape, or before, or both. If she is still with her abuser, she will originally have gone there for another reason, officially. The possibility of her speaking out to a professional is likely to worry the abuser and professionals should always be aware that he may sabotage the victim's progress.

There are different kinds of therapy, including:

- Individual therapy – Involves only the patient and the therapist.
- Couples' therapy – This therapy helps spouses and partners understand why their loved one has problems, what changes in communication and behaviours can help, and what they can do to cope. Abusers may consent to undertake couples therapy, but will be wary of honestly admitting what has happened. All concerned should be aware that therapy without honesty is a waste of time, and may be damaging. Health professionals must be vigilant for signs of deception and should try to maintain honesty within the sessions.
- Family therapy – This therapy allows the family unit to operate as a small group, in therapy. It is sometimes helpful for family members to understand how they themselves can cope and what they can do to help.
- Group therapy – Here two, three or more patients may participate in therapy at the same time. Patients are able to share experiences and learn that others feel the same way and have had the same experiences.

'Sufferers will regain a sense of control and pleasure in life.'

Therapy aims to help sufferers understand the behaviours, emotions, ideas, life problems or events, and helps them to understand which of those problems they may be able to solve or improve. The overall aim is that sufferers will regain a sense of control and pleasure in life, as well as learning coping techniques and problem-solving skills. Doctors sometimes prescribe medication such as antidepressants to accompany therapy. (Foa et al, 2009)

Medication

A sufferer may well find herself prescribed something like Prozac (fluoxetine). This works well for most people, but not for all. We are individuals. All medication has some side effects and some people may find that the side effects are too much to bear. It is very important to be honest with your doctor about this.

Tranquillisers such as Valium (diazepam) are described as minor tranquillisers, but are not minor in effect. While they may work well, they have been found to be highly addictive and fear of withdrawal symptoms when it is time to stop them has meant that many people stay on them for much longer than they should.

It is important to take only medication that has been prescribed for you personally, and to keep talking to your doctor about its effects while you take it. The wrong tablet (for you) can easily make life worse, clouding your judgement and taking away your ability to make sensible decisions, or even to act at all. Always be wary of the possible effects of medication and continue to talk about them to trusted health professionals, who should always listen seriously to complaints about side effects.

Identifying the problem

The main aim of talking to someone about problems is that the victim can begin to find their own way back towards health. The first step is 'admitting there is a problem'. The climate of denial that the victim has lived in for so long is the first major stumbling block. That there are problems may be obvious to outsiders, but the victim has used all her energy for so long trying to 'paper over the cracks'. She is ashamed of her situation and has accepted her abuser's word that everything is her fault. She believes she has failed and that she deserves her situation.

'She believes she has failed and that she deserves her situation.'

When, however, she finds that someone will allow her space just to be herself, the ground is prepared for the possibility of talk. She must find this space long before she can begin to trust or allow herself to be listened to.

Identifying the problem is not as straightforward as it may seem to an outsider. Someone listening to a victim might find it difficult and frustrating that she refuses to admit to the real problems, but there really is no way around it. As Maria* explained, 'I could not see that there might be a way out of my nightmare. I was sure I was trapped there forever. I don't know really what made the difference. I had begun to talk to Sylvia* a little bit and, one day, the flood gates opened. I suddenly saw that there was a door and I might walk through it. Of course I didn't leave immediately – not for a long time. I wasn't brave enough. But at least I could see that it was there, that there might be another way of life.'

Identifying the problem is not something someone else can do for you. But someone (friend or professional) who has good listening skills can go a long way towards helping create a place where the victim can begin to see what she might do. When she identifies the problem for herself, the scene is set for life to move on.

Seeing the light

Bob* described his life as a 'trap' and, even years later, could never identify the trigger that had made him realise he could change his situation. The day that someone begins to 'see the light' about life and its possibilities may not be dramatic or well defined. The victim might come to the point of despair, realise that she simply 'can't go on' and may believe that suicide is the only way out of the trap, and make an attempt on her own life. Or she might come to a different thought – where it suddenly occurs to her that she is 'worth more than this'.

'Once we have seen the light, life will never be the same again.'

Jackie* described the day when her three-year-old daughter suggested they should leave and her shame at having to be told this by a little child. She still did not find a way to actually leave for another six or seven months. She needed (as many people do) to work up to that day.

The world of domestic violence is full of fear and denial. Even when there is no immediate threat, the habit of fear has become overwhelming and prevents us from seeing what our life has become, and how to change it. But once we have seen the light, life will never be the same again.

Scenario

Loren* had all the defences in place that she could find. Her husband had always made it plain that he would not tolerate her speaking to anyone about their life. He said that he would kill her if she did, and she believed him. Because of this constant threat, she had established all the necessary changes in her life that prevented her from ever slipping into talking to someone. She kept her guard up against the rest of the world, because she did not want to put herself at risk from his anger by mistake.

But the feeling that she must talk to someone began to grow inside her. One day, she found herself in a strange part of town, not knowing how she had got there. She panicked. Was she going mad? What had happened to her? How could she explain where she had been to her husband?

She found herself in tears on a public street, with no one to turn to. A woman passing by asked if she was alright and Loren* began to shake. The woman bought her a coffee and let her use her mobile to phone the Samaritans. They gave her the number for Women's Aid. She was given the address of the drop-in centre and a few weeks later, managed to go there. What might happen next?

Summing Up

- Talking to someone about the facts of your life is the only way to begin to change. It is not easy to find a safe place or person to talk honestly to, but it can be done. Partners are not all-seeing and there are times when a conversation may be allowed to happen outside the home.
- Therapists sometimes refer to the 'strangers on a train' phenomenon, where a conversation takes place with someone we know we will never see again. This principle underlies telephoning helplines such as Women's Aid or the Samaritans. One big problem with these (wonderful) sources of help is that the abuser may well check the phone bills, looking at every number dialled and demanding to know who they are. Violence will then follow. While a personal pay-as-you-go phone, unknown to the abuser, would provide an answer to this, these cost money which the victim probably does not have.
- If a woman can find herself free in the vicinity of a Women's Aid drop-in centre, she will find a welcome and a listening ear that help immensely. Unfortunately, it is difficult to discover where these are and often difficult to get to them without arousing the abuser's suspicions. But victims sometimes become very creative in finding ways around these problems, and once they have found a way, they begin to grow again in secret, until the moment comes that they are strong enough to leave.

'Partners are not all-seeing.'

Chapter Four

Family

Family values

When we speak of family values, we think of a good support network made up of people who care about each other, who are ready to listen to each other and offer support. Of course, this is not always the case. All families have some problems, and these can take many forms. We learn about the world and our place in it from what we experience of family in our early years – the 'attachment bonds' and patterns that we establish.

'People who have never experienced violence sometimes state that they would not 'go under' to its effects, but they are wrong.'

Victims do not necessarily come from broken homes or dysfunctional families. Many have had happy childhood experiences, which cause the arrival of violence and abuse to be a totally unexpected shock, at all levels. A happy background only means that sudden violence is completely incomprehensible. Equally, victims who have suffered from growing up in a troubled family already have private doubts about their own place in the world and are very easily emotionally destroyed, however well they conceal their uncertainties. People who have never experienced violence sometimes state that they would not 'go under' to its effects, but they are wrong. Either way, the sudden onset of violence in a relationship is devastating, and no one is immune from its effects.

Experts speak of 'attachment bonds', when they discuss what we have learned from our families. People seek increased attachment in the face of danger. Adults, as well as children, may develop strong emotional ties with people who intermittently harass, beat and threaten them. Violence can be repeated on behavioural, emotional and physical levels. This leads to a confusion of pain and love. Repetition causes a large variety of suffering. Attachment problems are those with relationship boundaries, lack of trust and social isolation. Sufferers may have difficulty responding to other's emotional states.

Victims of domestic violence often suffer as a result from a fair amount of anger, directed against themselves, which arises from the sense of powerlessness that the situation brings. This is also true for those who have been helpless witnesses to violence, especially children. Many people reconsider the events over and over again in their minds, as they try to come to terms with events. They come to regard themselves as bad people, or accept the label 'out of control'. But regaining control over life, rather than reliving its disasters, is the real goal.

Children

Children also have attachment needs and are routinely distressed or unhappy about minor things that soon pass. Unfortunately, parents who have suffered domestic violence may find it difficult to respond to their needs in a sensitive way. This difficulty could have adverse repercussions for their children's social and emotional development.

One result in both children and adults, may be to seek increased attachment to people, even to caregivers who inflict pain, and children may confuse love and pain, with serious repercussions in later life. In children and adolescents this can have serious effects on their social and emotional development, as well as on their ability to learn. Shirley* described how her toddler suffered severe constipation, which stopped miraculously as soon as they left Shirley's* husband. She believed that she had kept the facts from her daughter, but it seemed that the child was much more aware of events than Shirley realised. After leaving, however, if the little one saw a can of Special Brew on the street, she would start to howl in terror. This behaviour stopped after a while.

Children may re-experience trauma through repeated play that has violence-related themes and distressing dreams, instead of through memories. As with adults, children may show re-experiencing symptoms. These include avoidance symptoms, where the child feels 'numb'. Or hyperarousal may be present and may cause significant distress or social and learning problems. Children may also have difficulty identifying and expressing their emotions, as well as difficulties communicating needs, wants and wishes. Children – like adults – may also suffer from dissociation and a lack of behavioural control, as well as problems with their self-image.

Children and adolescents can also be helped by listening therapies, but it is important to first identify the truth about the family background. If violence is involved, the young person is just as much caught up in the 'secrets and lies' as anyone else behind those closed doors. Anyone working with a young person must first find a way to establish a relationship 'bridge', in which the child can begin to trust. This is far from easy. We must carefully decide when and how to address traumatic memories.

Therapists use play with younger children and creative approaches such as writing and artwork as children become older. Work with any child should be done in conjunction with meeting the caregiver's needs. The road to health is not straightforward for anyone, and within a family a fine balance must be maintained so that no individual is left behind, which could cause new problems for other family members. Continuation of distressing family circumstances must be resolved.

A family affair

'The road to health is not straightforward for anyone.'

We can see, then, that nothing happens in a family that is truly private, however much we try to keep it secret. Physical violence may only occur after the children are asleep or out of the way, but they will still know that things are badly wrong, and this will affect their health and abilities. It will also affect how they learn to deal with the rest of the world.

When – not if – children begin to display problems at school, a teacher may become concerned and ask to talk to the mother. This is a difficult moment. As a parent you do not know the teacher well enough to confide in her, but she does offer a link to services that might begin to help the family. How much you disclose is a big problem. Many mothers lie about home life at this point, because they are afraid that social services will become involved and their child will be taken away from them.

One way forward is to listen carefully to what the teacher says and asks, and agree to give it some thought. Then ask if you can meet her again, to talk about things. This will please her, since you have listened fully to what she says, and she will feel that she has made progress. She will observe your child with a more sympathetic eye until you meet again, and will be happy to offer her thoughts and observations. Because trust is a two-way street and listening skills do not only belong to professionals, you are already beginning to build a relationship with someone who may be able to help.

It is hard to know how much of this to tell to an abusive partner. He or she will be furious and may even threaten to make trouble for the teacher who has involved herself in 'private business'. Since this is a likely worry, you might want to mention to her that your husband/partner 'has a temper', as soon as possible, so she will be more ready for any angry outbursts from him.

'A mother can convey, by looks and gestures, that she wants help for her child.'

So the decision to tell a partner is tricky and personal. On balance, it is probably best to mention that you have met with the teacher, even though it will probably result in violence. But that is going to be true whenever he finds out. So it might be better to do this sooner rather than later. Later would give him 'proof' of deception that he always looks for. He may insist on coming to the second meeting, but the teacher will then be able to observe that he is controlling and possibly unreasonable and that the family has something to hide, without too much being said. A mother can convey, by looks and gestures, that she wants help for her child, even when her husband/partner is loudly objecting.

Quietly saying thank you to the teacher at the end of this discussion will encourage her to make matters more official. While this may seem to be a terrible way to proceed, and abusive spouses will always see it as total disloyalty, this may be the only chance to take family problems to a wider audience, where someone can offer help to more than just the children. (Cook et al, 2005)

Scenario

Rachel's* two children, both under school age, were beginning to learn about life. The boy was aggressive in his approach to the world, and particularly began to spit at and punch his sister and his mother. The little girl became increasingly quiet and withdrawn. Rachel* tried to reason with her boy, but he did not listen, and she began to despair. Her daughter was growing up 'thinking that this was how it was for women', and her son was copying his father.

Although she 'didn't care about herself', Rachel* knew something had to change before her children were damaged.

What should she do? How could she stop the damage? Who might help her towards a way to find help for her children?

Summing Up

- Within any family, the members are always intertwined with each other in hundreds of ways. There are no ready answers to family problems, and when they are rooted in violence – and possibly drink – a lot is invested in keeping the truth from public eyes. (Humphreys, Gorard, 2009)
- It is not uncommon to hear abused women say that they 'don't care about themselves', because they have been told for so long that they are worthless and have no rights or status. The realisation that others need help (especially our children) can, however, be the trigger. This may begin the move towards getting help and support. Abuse is serious and creates long-term problems for all concerned. It must be recognised for what it is, and the secrets that keep it in place must be exposed.

Chapter Five

Post-traumatic Stress Syndrome

Definition

You may have heard of post-traumatic stress syndrome or disorder (PTSD). There is no doubt that if you are abused you will show some of the symptoms. Violence is chronic (long-lasting) and therefore causes changes in our thinking and physical responses to life.

'A lot is invested in keeping the truth from public eyes.'

The word 'post' signifies 'following'. Traumatic refers to injury – repetitive and chronic, in this case. Stress is a word that we all use quite a lot now. It simply describes the consequence of failure to respond appropriately to threats, which may be emotional as well as physical. A syndrome is a collection of signs and symptoms. Post-traumatic stress syndrome/disorder (PTSD) is therefore a collection of signs and symptoms that we develop, following a lengthy time of trauma or abuse.

Signs and symptoms

Symptoms of PTSD include nervousness, irritability, exhaustion, muscular tension, inability to concentrate, and features such as headaches and raised blood pressure or heart rate.

There are actually two definitions, one more precise than the other. One of these is complex post-traumatic stress disorder (C-PTSD). C-PTSD better describes the pervasive negative nature of chronic repetitive trauma than does PTSD alone (Judith Herman,1997). The category is however not formally recognised in diagnostic systems, so expect professionals to discuss symptoms simply as PTSD.

These elements include:

- Captivity – or a sense of being trapped.
- Psychological fragmentation.
- Disempowerment – the loss of a sense of safety, trust, and self-worth.
- The tendency to be re-victimised.
- Loss of a sense of self.

Trauma may be physical or mental, but in domestic violence it is almost always both. Women are twice as likely as men to develop PTSD, but of course men are abused too, and it should never be assumed that only women suffer. Virtually any trauma (defined as an event that is life-threatening or that severely compromises the emotional wellbeing of an individual or causes intense fear) may cause PTSD.

Although not all individuals who have been abused develop PTSD, there are usually significant physical consequences. Women who were also sexually abused at earlier ages are more likely to develop complex PTSD.

Babies that are born to mothers who suffered PTSD during pregnancy are more likely to experience a change in at least one chemical in their body. This makes it more likely that the baby will develop PTSD or ADHD (see glossary) later in life.

Individuals who suffer from PTSD are at risk of having more medical problems, as well as trouble becoming pregnant. Sufferers sometimes struggle more to achieve as good an outcome from mental health treatment as that of people with other emotional problems. Untreated PTSD has devastating, far-reaching consequences for sufferers' functioning and relationships, their families, and for society. (National Institute of Mental Health, 2011)

There are three major groups of symptoms:

- Recurrent re-experiencing of the trauma. This includes troublesome memories, flashbacks that are usually caused by reminders of the traumatic events, nightmares, etc).
- A numbing of emotional responses, even a phobia of places, people, noises and experiences that recall of the trauma.
- Hyperarousal and hyper vigilance to threat, including trouble concentrating, irritability, anger, sleep problems, poor concentration, blackouts or difficulty remembering things, increased tendency and reaction to being startled.

Other symptoms are:

- Somatisation – Where mental pain is felt as actual pain in the body, commonly stomach ache, headache, neck or back pain and so on.
- Alterations in systems of meaning – We all assign meanings to objects but in this stage, what an object means to us is changed, usually appearing more sinister because of its associations. For instance, in domestic violence, an object used to hit someone (perhaps a cricket bat) may become terrifying – or even the sound of a bat upon a ball, in a perfectly innocent setting. Changes in your system of meanings may also include a loss of sustaining faith or an overwhelming sense of hopelessness and despair.

'They may escape from one violent or abusive situation, only to find themselves drawn into another.'

Adults with C-PTSD have sometimes experienced prolonged trauma as children, as well as prolonged trauma as adults. This interrupts the development of a sense of self and of others. Physical and emotional pain or neglect was often inflicted by 'attachment figures', such as caregivers or older siblings, and as a result these individuals may develop a sense that they are fundamentally flawed and that others cannot be relied upon. Traumatised people also seem to be at risk for higher use of alcohol, cigarettes, marijuana and heavier drugs.

Individuals with complex PTSD sometimes also demonstrate lasting personality disturbances with a significant risk of re-victimisation. They may escape from one violent or abusive situation, only to find themselves drawn into another. There is no doubt that this is a risk and it is this tendency that makes it difficult for others (outsiders) to understand or sympathise with the problem. It is a pattern that must be broken, however long it takes.

Firstly, it is important to recognise that re-victimisation is a symptom of abuse. We can quickly be given a completely new (and wrong) view of ourselves as worthless human beings. While this is an easy thing for someone to impose upon us (even the strongest of us) it is a harder thing to change back that any outsider can imagine. We may not even realise how deeply the experience of abuse has changed us. But what is important to recognise first is that the 'deeply changed you' will respond to people and situations in new ways. One of these ways may include drifting into situations that turn out to be repetitions of an abusive or violent situation.

Breaking free

So can we deal with all this? Yes.

'No one is doomed to repeat their mistakes forever.'

No one is doomed to repeat their mistakes forever, but you must recognise that you have changed, and the 'way back' is a long, hard haul. Recognise the problems first (and the symptoms) and then you can begin work on changing your mind and your outlook right back again.

Emotional responses may be altered. There is no doubt that you may always be left with some changes and uncertainties. For instance, you may regain trust, but it may be many years before you believe that others trust you, and factors such as this will affect how you deal with the rest of the world.

Alterations may have occurred in attention or consciousness. Attention may become a problem. The sufferer appears to be distracted by thoughts that do not relate to conversation or the job in hand. It is important to deal with this problem systematically. It is alright to say – when having trouble with this, 'Sorry, my mind was elsewhere. I'm not thinking straight today.' A smile and a few words will allow you to pause the conversation and get back on track.

Alterations in self-perception include a sense of helplessness, shame, guilt, stigma and a sense of being completely different from other human beings. Eating and sleeping disorders may surface here and, of course, the loss of self-esteem and self-worth that accompanies all domestic violence. Variations in consciousness may occur, such as forgetting or reliving traumatic events.

These alterations must be recognised for the symptoms that they are and it is a good idea to share these feelings with someone else, preferably a professional.

Sufferers may also have episodes of dissociation (feeling 'detached' from your mental processes or body). This also includes alterations in relations with others. Because of the (now established) belief that we are no longer worthy, lovable and so on, we cease to relate to others and retreat into a compensating or defensive persona.

This is simply an attempt to move away from potentially hurtful situations (and relationships) but of course can quickly become a trap of its own and should be tackled as quickly as possible. Changes may occur in perception of the perpetrator. Victims may attribute total power to the perpetrator or become preoccupied with the relationship – even thinking of revenge. Again, all these feelings should be shared with a professional.

The changes in yourself may mean that the way back to health is blocked at first, because of them. Reflecting honestly upon them is vital. To see that your attitude has changed is to realise that there is something that needs work.

'Reflecting honestly . . . is vital.'

There are recognised approaches which help someone suffering from PTSD and these should happen under the guidance of a qualified professional. However, there are also things that a sufferer can do to help herself towards health. Both of these will be discussed in a later chapter. For now, believe that it can be done, and look at yourself as honestly as possible.

If observations can be shared with a professional, guidance can be given. If, however, you find yourself without professional support, a diary is a good place to record items. Putting thoughts and concerns down in black and white is therapeutic, but also gives a baseline to work from and to record improvements. Many people keep an online journal or blog and may be linked in to a particular group of people suffering (or recovering) in the same way. John* and Natasha* both found this particularly helpful and many other victims have felt the benefit. Communities also give you the chance to be helpful to others, which is massively therapeutic. However, *do* use a pseudonym and take steps to keep your real identity and location secret. It would not be good to attract further problems.

Recovery from C-PTSD occurs in three stages. These are:

- Re-establishing safety.
- Remembrance and mourning for what has been lost.
- Reconnecting with the community and society.

Some experts believe that recovery can only occur within a healing relationship, and only if the survivor is empowered by that relationship. This may look like an impossible goal, but it is achievable. One of the first things to remember about this is that it may not be a relationship with a man. A child, a group, a friend, a job – all of these can give you the positive emotional feedback necessary to rebuild life and persona.

Exercise

Take some time to describe yourself, warts and all. For instance, if you are particularly nervous, especially in relation to certain situations, list it here.

What kind of humour do you use?

Is there a cruel edge to it?

Describe yourself *before* you came into your current relationship.

Draw the comparisons.

Is there anything that you feel you must now claim back into your life?

Summing Up

- PTSD can be cured, and ways to health will be discussed later. For now it is important to know that you can identify the changes in yourself, by allowing yourself to recognise that post-traumatic stress syndrome has invaded your life. This is as a direct result of the domestic violence that you have suffered, and this recognition is the next stage in your way back to reclaiming your sense of self.
- Becoming yourself again is not easy, but you need to know that thousands of us have achieved it. Can I ever be the same as I once was? Maybe not. In fact, the chances are that you will be permanently changed by the years of domestic violence that trapped you for so long. The real question is – will those changes necessarily be bad ones? Here the answer must be *no*. The changes that you will find within yourself, once you have worked through the necessary issues, are almost all good, positive ones. It is easy, however, to divert from good outcomes into bad traps, at any point of the way. Stay with it and you will find the way to return to yourself. If this is not to the person you once were, it may be to the person that you were born to be, with all the strength, goodness and benefits that can bring. (Foa et al, 2009)

'Can I ever be the same as I once was?'

For more information on PTSD see *Post-traumatic Stress Disorder – The Essential Guide* (Need2Know).

Chapter Six

Self-Esteem

Needs

It is important to recognise that needs and wants are very different things. We may believe that something we want – perhaps very badly – is in fact something we need. This is not so.

As far back as 1954, the psychologist Abraham Maslow published his description of his work on 'needs'. He aimed to show that some needs were the most basic and others were those that we aspire to. Usually, these are described as a triangle, with the most essential forming the base, although Maslow did not use a triangular shape in his original work.

The most basic needs described by Maslow, are those essential to life. These include air, food, drink, shelter, sleep, warmth, etc. There is no doubt that these are the needs that anyone must have – and yet sometimes victims of violence may be deprived of some of these. The needs that follow these basics in Maslow's 'hierarchy' are those concerned with safety. These include limits and boundaries, security, stability and protection. Here we are definitely in an area where victims experience a lack. The abuser's need to control them and the situation in general means that he will deprive her of these essentials. Already the victim is being deprived of her basic human rights and needs.

'The abuser's need to control them and the situation in general means that he will deprive her of these essentials.'

Promotion of self-esteem

Beyond these absolute basics, Maslow goes on to describe those needs that centre around self-esteem. These are love and belonging, self-esteem and self-actualisation, wherein an individual can reach their personal potential as a human being. These are essential to becoming a healthy, well-rounded person, but cannot be achieved unless the first two sets of needs are in place, which is probably why it has become popular to describe Maslow's 'hierarchy' as a triangle, with sets of needs building upon each other.

Love and belonging include needs such as family support, good relationships and a sense that we are loved and belong to a particular group. Again, we can see how an abused individual is deprived of these essentials. Without them, the growth of self-esteem, which is the core of good mental health, is impossible. These give us the core of a sense of identity.

When we move on from the abusive situation, it is important that we find people and situations who can give us this. Actual esteem needs, according to Maslow, include a sense of responsibility and achievement. How do we find these? There as many ways forward as there are individuals, but a remarkable number of people describe the act of helping someone else (a friend, their children, etc.) to feel better about life as essential, here.

'The sense of being 'lost' is as emotionally crippling as the fear that a victim lives with.'

'Self-actualisation' sounds like a difficult concept, but in fact only means becoming the best person that you can be. It grows out of putting the other needs in place. Here, individuals are described as becoming creative, having a sense of humour and so on. These features may seem distant to a victim who is still in the domestic violence trap. But as they break free and begin to emerge as themselves, they will find that their capacity for these things grows.

Lost and found

To be deprived of the basic essentials, as described by Maslow, is to feel very lost and alone. The needs in this classic list are those which allow someone to see herself as an individual, in her own right.

The sense of being 'lost' is as emotionally crippling as the fear that a victim lives with. Without that sense of identity, we feel that we are so lost we cannot even find anything to hold on to. There is nothing to provide an anchor and we are swept around feeling helpless and hopeless.

The only way to reach any kind of 'safer' place, where we might 'find' ourselves again, is to begin to reach out to another human being and to talk to them. It has been so long since we risked doing this, that this is in itself a massive step. Courage is needed, and that is hard to come by.

But what is there to lose? Try it. Allow yourself to let someone help. This is the way that a victim can begin to 'find' herself again.

Who do you think you are?

This is the moment that a victim should reconsider who she is. It may well be that she begins this process by just reflecting and daydreaming. Probably when someone begins this process, they will find that there are many features that they no longer like about themselves, but it is important that these are faced and examined, before they can be dealt with.

Exercise

(Children's crayons are recommended for this exercise.)

Begin by continuing to describe your situation as it is now – both good things and bad things. You may struggle to think of things to say about yourself, but one good way to begin is to draw a picture of yourself. You do *not* have to be an artist! A stick image will do, but add in colour and cartoon features. Children's crayons are *very* good for this. Use your non-dominant hand.

Amuse yourself by doing this and then add in the words that go with the features in your picture. Allow yourself to laugh at yourself and your efforts.

Now draw yourself again, as you would like to be. Allow yourself to imagine things that might seem impossible, but perhaps are based upon the person you have already drawn. Some of the words used to describe yourself in the first drawing may simply be reversed. Make this as jokey and as silly as you like. Add in words and colour, if you are drawing.

Repeat again tomorrow, or very soon.

Keep the words and drawings. They are an important part of you.

'Allow yourself to let someone help.'

Summing Up

- The key to regaining self-esteem – and good mental health – is to be honest about a situation, ourselves and our needs. If we can find ways of keeping that honesty, we are going to win the battle. There is no doubt that a loss of self-esteem has been a major part of what has kept you in the domestic violence trap. Make the resolution not to let this continue into your future, damaging this as it has damaged your past. Enough is enough.
- When we look at ways of improving self-esteem, the most effective remedies are those that have some basis in creativity. Many people believe themselves to be completely uncreative and that they need some kind of talent to do this. That is not true. Creativity is anything that offers a kind of emotional release. The point about any creative activity is the sense of freedom from our adult roles that it can bring. If something makes us chuckle or think of something new, it is creative in its nature – even if we are spectators rather than actually acting. (Butler, 2010; Leveton 2010)

'If we can find ways of keeping that honesty, we are going to win the battle.'

Chapter Seven

Good Health

What keeps us well?

Firstly, it is important to recognise the things that make us less than healthy. There are many such factors and by this stage you will have already thought about some of those. The sense of being trapped and controlled, constant fear, lack of ways in which to express or enjoy yourself and so on.

The things that keep (or make) us well are the opposites of these. Finding things that remove the sense of being trapped is first on the list. Here, however, it would be very easy to fall into another trap, where drugs or alcohol are used. These are not solutions. They only lead very quickly to other – massive – problems. You will never be free if you swap an unhappy lifestyle for addiction or dependence.

'Find something to do – however briefly – that has been forbidden by the abuser.'

Instead, the answer is to find something to do – however briefly – that has been forbidden by the abuser. This must of course be something that you enjoy, but need not be anything dramatic or cost money. Just sitting in a favourite place, perhaps watching the children play, or listening to your own type of music, can meet this need. It is important, however, to do this consciously and also to consciously think 'I am doing this; you (the abuser) would be furious if you could see me!' and to allow yourself to laugh about that, because he cannot stop you anymore.

The constant mistrust that is part of an abusive relationship takes a heavy toll on a victim. Towards the end of their time in such a relationship, many women begin to think and fantasise about having an affair. This is also not a good plan, since it can lead to so much more that will cause further damage. Above all, affairs mess up our emotions even further and damage our personal perceptions. Keep the reward of a new sexual relationship for after leaving, once you have a clearer head. It is easier to spot the bad guys with a clear head.

Once you have identified the habits and factors that keep you trapped – and therefore make you less than well – you can start to take control of them and begin the process of reversal.

Physical health

Good physical health spins off from improved mental health. It is impossible to separate the two, so everything that improves physical health will help mental health and vice versa.

Good physical health centres around diet and exercise, but this is not to say that anyone who is not ready to exercise or change their diet should push at these. But as with other ways to change, the first step is to think about change. Food that is cheap – which may therefore seem necessary – is often not very good or nutritious. But there are exceptions to this. Eggs and cheese are terrific sources of nutrition, as are all kinds of meat, fruit and vegetables. Avoid fat and fry-ups.

High calorie foods that offer a sense of being full (briefly) and offer no nutrition can bring comfort, but will only contribute to a feeling of tiredness when you really need to be alert and beginning to work through a whole new set of issues. These are best avoided.

Smoking, drinking and drugs are not good for anyone, and cost money that could be better spent elsewhere. Try to give up.

There is no ideal diet to keep us healthy, and diets that claim to be the answer to everything are not really helpful. It is possible to change our attitude to food and to think of every item in terms of its potential to help or damage your health, and then to make choices based on that. Many people who live with a controlling partner find that a certain type of food has been denied them for a long time. But now it is possible to eat – and take pleasure from – those things. Of course, an excess of junk food is a bad thing, but an occasional treat is good. And if something that is good for you has been prohibited, now is a good time to get both the physical and psychological benefits of rediscovering it.

Diet cannot be separated from exercise. Again, this need not be massive, or cost very much. Walking is free and saves money on bus fares. It has been suggested that any exercise is even more beneficial if it is carried out in the open air and especially so in a green space. A variety of route can also help to stimulate the mind.

Any movement is better than none, and we should aim for at least a short brisk walk every day. When we move we improve metabolism, which helps food to digest and to be better used.

It is said that the three best exercises are walking, swimming and cycling. Walking costs nothing. Cycling involves the cost and maintenance of a bicycle. Swimming memberships can be found in many places at reasonable rates and may include classes such as aqua-aerobics and aqua-zumba (which are great fun and do not need any swimming ability!) in the price or, if they are linked to a gym membership, classes such as Pilates or kick boxing. The trick here is to work out how often you need to use your membership in a week, so that each session is in fact costing very little and can be justified within a very tight budget.

'Physical and mental health cannot be clearly separated.'

And all of these are good things to do with children. Family life always benefits from activities done together. One of the first benefits in doing something active, that you enjoy, is that you start to smile again. It may be some time since you felt free enough to smile – or even laugh – and at this point, any type of exercise begins to benefit mental health too. The company of others has been denied for so long, that just conversations with others can have immense benefits.

We are told that physical and mental health cannot be clearly separated, because physical activity releases brain chemicals called endorphins, which keep low mood and depression at bay. While a doctor may offer antidepressants to someone who has suffered for a long time, it is much better if the body can produce its own chemicals, rather than relying on an intake of drugs (or alcohol) that may lead to the additional problems of addiction.

How to promote good mental health

By the time that someone has found a way to escape the bad situation, a great deal has already been achieved. It is important to recognise this, and to feel proud of the achievement. Starting with exercise ideas, as described above, it is possible to build upon this progress.

The next best way to improve mental health is to do something creative. No talent is needed! To enjoy music, and to get the benefit of that enjoyment, doesn't mean that we have to be able to play an instrument. We only need to be able to spend some time listening to a favourite radio station, where the music and the mood is the one that we enjoy. Reading can allow us to escape everyday life and library membership costs nothing. (Libraries often also offer information about events or activities in the community, which may also cost nothing at all.)

'She no longer had to worry that there would be repercussions if she chatted with others.'

Cheap paper and crayons can allow us to make elaborate and colourful doodles that are great fun and give an unexpected sense of achievement. Try not to worry about creating art – just concentrate on having fun. Allow yourself to build more and more elaborate drawings and designs, but don't worry about realism. Drawing and painting are not photography and it is self-expression that gives the pleasure factor. Billie* liked some of hers so much that she bought a few second-hand picture frames to display them on her wall and to be additionally proud of herself.

Piara* described her surprise when she realised that what her new life offered was conversation. She no longer had to worry that there would be repercussions if she chatted with others. Passing the time of day with strangers became something that she actively tried to do. And she knew that sometimes she had brightened someone else's day (especially the elderly) who she realised might be lonely and also suffering from a lack of human contact.

Sarah* realised that she could only afford clothes (and other items) from charity shops, but was pleased and happy to find how good these could be. She even decided to volunteer at one of them, one morning a week, and gained a surprising psychological boost from this.

Sam* discovered his local MIND drop-in centre and offered his help there as a volunteer, which eventually led to a whole new career. Other survivors describe benefits from helping at the local mothers and toddlers group, Samaritans or as classroom assistants. Local libraries have contact lists of places to volunteer and all of these groups offer a sense of belonging, conversation and ways to feel better. (If you think volunteering might be for you, take a look at *Volunteering – The Essential Guide* Need2Know)

Magda* discovered (via the library) a course that she could take, which interested her and which she could afford. She came away with a certificate, a new set of skills and a number of new friends who shared her interest. These outlets and activities all help to improve positive 'self regard' – wherein we begin to feel better about ourselves.

Positive self-regard

'There is no overnight cure for the depths of despair that victims endure.'

Positive self-regard means that the way we view ourselves moves from being negative, where we can only see the unhappy parts of life and may believe bad things about ourselves, to a place where it is possible to see good things and to begin to build life around them.

To actually reach a state of positive self-regard is going to take a long time, but every step of the way towards that state is rewarding. There is no overnight cure for the depths of despair that victims endure. But there are ways of helping positive self-regard to grow.

The first item necessary to the growth of positive self-regard is personal space. It is very possible to find that, having escaped, the place you must live is not attractive and has problems that may well contribute to lowering mood. But this can be approached in two ways. Firstly, anything that can be improved on – either by yourself or by the landlord should be tackled. Secondly, this is your space. It is important to remember that the door can be closed on the rest of the world and that this space can be made more comfortable by adding in the personal items that matter to you. This is a place where the creative and relaxing activities discussed previously can take place. Organise your place to allow for these. If there is a limit to what you can do in your space, it is important to find somewhere – perhaps part of the local community centre – where what you want to do can be accessed for a few hours a week.

Positive self-regard is essentially what it says – a positive way of viewing yourself. Anything that might contribute to this, but which does not harm, is good. It is important to start to feel proud, and – if a blog or a journal is kept – this is one way of charting progress.

Of course, depression and the other results of PTSD may be overwhelming. It is important to share your feelings with the doctor if it is difficult to foster positive self-regard. But remember that the more you can do (exercise, diet, interests, etc.) to move things along, the better. If treatments are needed and offered, they should be accepted. But because there is no absolute cure for anything, it is important to keep the identified activities and interests going as much as possible.

Treatments

'It is important to start to feel proud.'

When depression or the effects of PTSD are overwhelming, professionals offer various types of therapy, such as individual counselling, sensorimotor psychotherapy, cognitive behavioural therapy, desensitisation, family therapy and group therapy. None of these provide the magic wand we may be seeking, but do offer an emotional outlet, and a safe place to talk. Therapy is hard work, but well worth the effort. There are relationships between thoughts and feelings. Exploring common negative thoughts, developing alternative interpretations and practising new ways of looking at things can help massively.

PTSD is caused by extraordinary stress, rather than any sort of weakness. Inaccurate ideas about the illness can be dispelled and the shame they may feel about having it is dealt with. Treatments for PTSD include psychological and medical treatments, usually working together, aimed at teaching the person ways to manage symptoms. Individuals are asked to talk about their experiences and to explore and modify any inaccurate ways of thinking. Sufferers can learn how to manage their anxiety and anger and how to improve their communication skills. Relaxation techniques can be taught, which help sufferers to gain mastery over their emotional and physical symptoms. These treatments also involve practising learned techniques in real-life situations.

Families may also benefit from family counselling. This may include couples' counselling, parenting classes and conflict-resolution education. Sleep problems should be addressed and it is best if this is not done by using drugs, since a person who is stressed and vulnerable is at increased risk of developing a dependency.

Exercise

Time to make another list, or rather several. You may want to divide a piece of paper into certain sections for this one, because everything we do affects us at more than one level and they all link in to each other.

The section headings should be 'Food', 'Exercise', 'Activities', 'Helping', and 'Other People'. Into each section list the people and things that make you feel good about yourself. If this is difficult at first, think about things that have been making you feel bad over the last few years and reverse them. You may not be able to do all of the activities you list, or afford the food that is good, but put them down anyway, because when the day comes that you can find a way to include them in real life, you will have an even bigger sense of achievement. Include an area where you might like to volunteer. Helping others can give a massive boost.

Keep this set of lists and add to them when you can. Tick things off as you find that you can make them part of your daily life.

Keep this list pinned up where you can see it every day. After a while, you may want to write a new one, but keep the old for comparison. You are doing well, and this is a measure of your progress.

Summing Up

- Physical and mental health are closely linked to each other and both can always be improved. Any improvement in one will benefit the other. Both are necessary to cope with the new challenges of life and to find the energy needed to go forward. Escape from a bad situation becomes possible when we begin to find that energy, and the beginnings of self-belief. (Itzin et al, 2010)

'No one can change your negative feelings and beliefs for you.'

Chapter Eight
Escape

Changing your mind

A change of mind or attitude is the first step back to recovery and a new life. To escape the bad situation, you first need to realise that there is 'more to life than this' and that you deserve good things. You have been told again and again that you deserve only abuse, you have caused it. But this is not true.

No one can change your negative feelings and beliefs for you. This is something that needs work, all day and every day. There is no magic wand. Violence continues to be a part of life until we actually leave, and even then fear of violence is going to be part of life for a long, long time. So how do we begin to 'change our minds'?

The first emotion to allow yourself is resentment. For too long, you have listened to the abusive words that accompany beatings. The distress of this combination leaves you feeling completely hopeless and helpless. The trap has closed around you.

Obviously during a beating, you must concentrate on keeping damage to a minimum. You have learned that to fight back will only increase his violence. Our natural response to the nightmare is also to close down emotionally, as much as possible. The first step in changing your mind is to allow yourself anger. What he says about you is not true. He has no right to say this. You do not deserve to be treated in this way.

After a first beating

Phone the police, be seen by a doctor. Make statements and make sure that your injuries are documented. Prosecute.

If you are hit for the first time, do not assume that this will never happen again. It will. Speak to the police or someone else in authority. Then walk away from him forever, or get an injunction to keep him out. (See The Law at the end of the book).

After repeated beatings

Allow your anger and resentment at his treatment to grow in secret. Bullies who physically abuse others are cowards. Allow yourself to see him for what he is.

It will be a shock to him when he realises that you have escaped the trap his emotional cruelty has kept you in, so allow yourself to privately draw strength from your anger and resentment, and start to notice the change that this brings in yourself. You may always have prided yourself on being a strong person and a good wife and mother. So now you may feel that it must be wrong to be angry. But it is time to develop a sense that you have needs and rights too and that you have nothing to be ashamed of. (Courtois, 2009)

'He has damaged you and – if you have children – is damaging them too.'

He has damaged you and – if you have children – is damaging them too. Allow yourself to be angry about that, and stop worrying about whether he is hurt by your change of heart.

Preparation

Now allow yourself to daydream a little. Earlier, an exercise asked you to think about the person you wanted to be when you were younger and had not yet met him. If you have not yet completed this exercise, go back to those pages, and do it now. Your first thought will probably be that there is no way you can return to being that person. But in fact, the person you were meant to be is still there inside you.

Whenever you have time and space, allow yourself to imagine the person you set out to be. This does not mean spending time on endless regret, although regret can help to fuel your anger. But take some time off from anger, and recognise the parts of you that are still hidden, deep in the core. Think of that part of yourself as an old and valued friend. Allow these thoughts to grow.

Most abusers keep their victims very short of money, since this is a classic way of keeping someone under control. You are already aware that he will check every penny and become furious if he finds anything out of place or unaccounted for. You have been scrupulously honest throughout because to be anything else is to ask for trouble. But now you need to acquire money, a little at a time.

If your man is a drinker, he will not know how much he has in his pocket at the end of a binge, but if you take some of this for yourself, you must be sure that it is never noticeable and never found. It is unlikely that you have a bank account in your own name and the last thing that you want is a statement coming to the house which shows him you have anything of your own. So what you do with any money you acquire is difficult. If he finds where you have it hidden, the consequences will be terrible – and he will take it back.

If you have a friend who would allow you to use her address temporarily for a bank account, so much the better. This again needs very careful thought.

Preparation is also about thinking through what you absolutely need in your life. What really matters? How to keep these things for yourself. What to let go, without regret.

'Life's essentials are much fewer than we might imagine.'

Essentials

Life's essentials are much fewer than we might imagine. Again we are looking at the difference between needs and wants. As we go through life, we tend to believe that we could never live without certain things. This is not true and now is the time to start imagining a good life, without those things. This can be quite liberating! You may want to start making a mental list of things that you really need and then checking a while later to see if it is true. All of your clothes are not essential to life, and you may come to realise that some are much more useful on a daily basis than others. If you have children, they have needs so a mental list for them, which includes some clothes, a favourite toy and perhaps something to read to them, would be a good idea. But then you will probably realise that a library card is a great thing and that libraries also provide a good comfortable place to spend some time, especially if your child is under school age.

The key to essentials is to ask yourself if it is something you could carry, alone, when the day comes that you decide to walk out – or if it can be substituted by something else. For this reason you will want to look at 'keeping it small'.

Keeping it small

As your list evolves, you will find that you consider things, and decide how easy – or not – it would be to take them with you. Most of us have a mobile phone, but if it is paid for by your husband or partner as part of his account, he will cancel it as soon as you leave, so it can't be used. If you acquire a little money, you may want to buy a pay-as-you-go phone just before you leave, which you can transfer contact numbers and information to. Leave your other mobile phone behind, having deleted any texts or numbers that might allow him to trace you. Delete any computer files that might help him too.

In some places it is possible to rent a small locker, such as 'left luggage' which you can pay for with the money you acquire and then all that you need to keep is a small key, which will never be noticed on your key ring. Into this, you can put certain things such as underwear and perhaps your money box. This is an especially good idea if you have items of sentimental value, such as family photographs, which would add to the bulk of things on the day you decide to go, but which would hurt very much to leave behind. Your passport, certificates or qualifications, driving licence, children's birth certificates and so on will all be needed and it is important that they are in a safe place ahead of time or taken with you when you leave. How you go about removing these from the family home, over time, is again something to be careful about. Never being found out is vital. Timing is everything.

You do need one or two items such as scissors, can opener, knives, forks, spoons and a couple of plates or (microwaveable) dishes as well. If you never manage to acquire locker space, these can easily be carried in a shoulder bag of a reasonable size. Depending on where you are moving to, dried food or cans could be included in the weekly shop and kept back for removal later. It is best that the bag that you use is one that you use a lot, for a while before you leave. You do not want to arouse his suspicions by making visible changes, so that he steps in and finds a way to destroy your plans.

Ready to walk

No one walks out on years of relationship easily. But the day comes when it becomes easier and now your preparations are made. Give yourself a little longer, so that you turn things over in your mind and make sure that there is nothing essential missing.

Keep a record – as precise as possible – of past events and any independent evidence, such as police reports or medical records. Include dates and times – if you have them – and all the effects on you and your children. You will need to make a sworn statement later to the court about the abuse you have experienced.

The turning point, when we find we can leave, is different for everyone. But there does come a day when enough is enough and it is time to go. If your preparations are in place, you will be able to take advantage of the energy that this day brings. On that day, it is as if we see things clearly and honestly for the first time.

'The turning point, when we find we can leave, is different for everyone.'

It would be easy to waste time and energy at this point being angry with yourself for not having moved on sooner. Please walk away from that sort of anger, which only uses up vital energy, and walk forward into the future.

Who you can share your secret with is something to be careful about. There are those among our friends who find it hard to believe that the situation is as we say it is, and who might misguidedly believe that they are helping by trying to create reconciliation. Professionals should be a good bet, because of their commitment to confidentiality, but this may not always be the case if they are also friends of the family or your partner. They are human beings, after all. Within the Asian community, women sometimes describe a certainty that their doctor will not respect confidentiality, and there have been known examples of 'bounty hunters' who will track down a woman for money. Of course, such a person would not hesitate to listen to hints from any source, however innocent. But it is important that someone knows your plans, so that help can be put into place.

Getting an injunction

A few decades ago, there was much less legal help for victims of violence, and women hesitated to contact the police because they expected a less sympathetic reception. This is no longer the case.

There are many older women who have never escaped from their situation, because when they were younger there was not as much to help and support them. (McGarry, Simpson; 2010). They still might find that they can change their lives, now. But again – the first step is realising that a change needs to be made and that they can make it. Edith* left her abusive husband when she was seventy and he was seventy-six. She died five years later, but often stated during that time that these were 'the best years of her life'.

An injunction may help. An injunction is a court order. Injunctions are normally for a specified period of time (perhaps six months) but can be renewed; or they may be made 'until further order'. There are two types of injunctions available under the Family Law Act 1996. These are:

- A non-molestation order.
- An occupation order.

A non-molestation order aims to prevent your partner or ex from using or threatening violence against you or your children. This includes intimidating, harassing or pestering you.

An occupation order regulates who can live in the family home and can also restrict your abuser from entering the surrounding area. If you have left home because of violence, but want to return and exclude your abuser, you can apply for an occupation order.

Getting a court order may provide some protection, but sometimes it makes very little difference and it can even be counterproductive.

In order to apply for one of these orders you must be an 'associated person'. This means that you must be at least one of these:

- You have been married to each other.
- You have been in a civil partnership with each other.
- You are cohabitants or former cohabitants (including same sex couples).

- You have lived in the same household.
- You are relatives.
- You have formally agreed to marry each other (even if that agreement has now ended).
- You have a child together.
- You are in an 'intimate relationship of significant duration'.
- You are both involved in the same proceedings (e.g. divorce or child contact).

If you are in immediate danger, an application can be made to the court on the same day without your abuser being there. This is called a 'without notice' or ex parte application. If the court grants a 'without notice' order, you will have to return to court for a full hearing once your abuser has been served with notice.

If you are being continually harassed, threatened or stalked after a relationship has ended, you can also get civil injunctions under the Protection from Harassment Act 1997. Restraining orders can provide the same protection as injunctions under the civil law, but may be more effective as they carry stronger penalties.

'Get a solicitor who has a lot of experience with domestic violence cases.'

Recent legislation also allows a restraining order to be attached when criminal proceedings have been taken, if the court believes you are likely to be at risk.

If you do not also need to apply for an injunction to exclude your abuser from your home, taking action under the criminal law (coupled with restraining orders) may help you avoid the cost of taking civil legal action.

If you are applying for an occupation order, the court will apply a 'balance of harm' test when deciding whether to make the order. The court may then make other related orders, for example, relating to repair and maintenance of the home, or to payment of rent or mortgage.

You can apply for an injunction yourself, but it is helpful to have legal advice. Get a solicitor who has a lot of experience with domestic violence cases. Your local Women's Aid organisation may be able to refer you to someone.

Applications for injunctions under the Family Law Act will be in a closed court, which means that no one not directly concerned with your case will be allowed in. You will be able to take in your solicitor, but not a friend – though one can wait for you in a waiting room. This provides a degree of privacy.

Court officers should also be able to provide separate waiting areas for you and your abuser. Ask for your address to be kept secret in court, so that the abuser does not know where you are staying.

The court sometimes suggests that, instead of an injunction, the abuser should make an undertaking to the court not to threaten you. This is supposed to have the same strength as a court order, but in practice undertakings cannot be enforced effectively, as powers of arrest cannot be attached. You do not have to agree to accept an undertaking if you do not want to.

Your solicitor must arrange for a printed copy of the injunction to be handed personally to your abuser. The injunction will not be effective if there is no proof that your abuser received it.

Under the Domestic Violence Crime and Victims Act 2004, breach of a non-molestation injunction will become a criminal offence. If he breaks the terms of the injunction, and you are at all fearful for your safety or that of others, you must call the police. Your abuser is in contempt of court for disobeying a court order. The court may then fine your abuser, impose a suspended sentence or even send him to prison. The court is also likely to add a power of arrest to the injunction in order to strengthen it in the future. (Buzawa et al, 2011)

Funding for legal action

If you are applying for legal aid to cover the costs of seeking protection from domestic abuse (e.g. a non-molestation order, occupation order or forced marriage protection order) then you will qualify for legal aid regardless of your income.

If you are on benefits or a low or no income and with little or no savings, you will not pay anything towards your legal costs.

If your income after essential outgoings (such as utility bills, mortgage or rent payments, and allowances for children) is over a certain amount, you will be asked to pay a contribution towards the costs of your case. You will also be asked to make a contribution if you have savings over a certain amount.

In the case of an urgent application for a domestic violence injunction, a solicitor who is contracted with the Legal Services Commission can grant an emergency certificate of legal representation.

See also the Citizens Advice Bureau, Court Service website and the Domestic Violence DIY Injunction Handbook, listed at the back of the book.

Refuge

Talking to Women's Aid may lead to the offer of a place in the local refuge, but the sad truth is that there are far more of us needing somewhere than there are ever spaces in the refuge. Places there are usually given to women with children, for whom escape would otherwise be impossible. Volunteers there can, however, be very helpful and supportive and may be able to suggest an alternative way forward.

'The address of the refuge must be kept secret.'

The address of the refuge must be kept secret, because no one wants irate husbands and partners turning up causing trouble for everyone. You must be prepared to help keep this secret, or the system would fall apart. Sometimes victims have a lingering hope that family problems can be resolved and that they will return to the family home. The refuge is not somewhere to go back to your husband or partner from. He will want to know where you have been. When that information is refused, he may well revert to patterns of violence, with obvious consequences and beat the information out of you.

Despite the help that Women's Aid can offer, many women still find they are afraid that the refuge will be a terrible place and imagine somewhere that is barely basic. They are always pleasantly surprised. The buildings are beautifully kept and facilities – although shared – are always clean and more than adequate.

This fear is expressed so often that we can see it easily becomes one of the barriers to escape for some women. Like all the other barriers, this is something that needs to be thought through. Making the decision to go to the refuge is quite a hard step, and once it has been taken you can congratulate yourself on being brave.

If a place is offered, there is no doubt that people consider you are seriously in need and you should allow yourself to go forward into the next stage of your life. Leaving an abusive spouse is not a sign of failure in any way. Quite the reverse. It is important not to dwell upon the past, but to see how the rest of your life can begin now, and that it is possible to become the person you were intended to be, rather than someone living in constant fear.

'It is important not to dwell upon the past.'

Exercise

Now make a list of the small things that it is absolutely essential you take with you, if you must leave your home at very short notice. Imagine that you have not had the chance to leave anything in a safe place. Looking at what you own, decide which bag would be the one with the best capacity to take with you. Remember not to leave an address book etc., where it can be found by your partner. Keep the list small.

Now double check to see if anything on this list can also be left behind.

Summing Up

- It is difficult to see a way out of the nightmare, when domestic violence is part of life. But it is important to realise that escape can happen. The biggest step is the realisation that it can be done, which then opens the door for planning and decisions as to what is essential in life.
- Everyone is individual in this. Making plans is the first step in taking control back, and the most important way to begin thinking about the sort of life that you want for yourself.

'Making plans is the first step.'

Chapter Nine

Scenarios and Exercises Discussed

Introduction – Exercise

This exercise asks you to think of someone you know, who might have needed help but did not really know how to ask for it. We can all look back and see that we should have asked more deeply and regret that, but it is a tricky situation. None of us get it quite right.

On the other hand, if you can recall the time when you wanted to reach out and ask someone for help, perhaps you can also look back and see now how you might have found a way to ask more of someone. What might they have said that would encourage you to say more? Perhaps you will find yourself able to help someone else in the future, if you let yourself look at these possibilities.

Chapter 1 – Scenario

There comes a day when a deteriorating relationship spills over into violence and nobody wants to believe that this will ever happen again, or that they fit the category of domestic abuse.

Unfortunately, once the line into violence has been crossed, it is impossible to go back. Neither party can ever see the other in quite the same light. The balance has shifted forever and, although the violent one may express guilt and remorse and promise that it will never happen again, they are extremely unlikely to be able to keep that promise.

Jane* found – as we all do – that it is harder to leave once the line has been crossed, unless she does it immediately and preferably also involves the police. Not acting at this point gives a psychological acceptance and already the issues become cloudy. The abuser may well feel some guilt, but this is often expressed as attempts at justification. 'You deserve this', 'You drove me to do that', 'See what you made me do'. We are all likely to take these statements on board, however unrealistic they are and, again, they help to reinforce acceptance of an unacceptable situation.

Chapter 2 – Scenario

This scenario expands upon the last one and highlights the belief that we must trust people in order to bring out the best in them and to avoid a repetition. Unfortunately, this is not true.

Joanne* needs to look at the pattern of their relationship and refuse to accept his behaviour. She must speak to someone official, police or medical, so that her experience is placed upon an official record.

It is unlikely that he will never do this again, if she stays, but an official record may make him hesitate. Should she need to go to court, the record is essential.

Chapter 3 – Scenario

Loren* came to a day when her living situation was simply too much for her. Because she was no longer emotionally equipped to help herself out of the problems, she had to find someone to talk to. For a woman, Women's Aid is the obvious first thought, closely followed by Samaritans. For men, there are are also helplines and organisations. Some helpful agencies aim to help specific groups (ethnic or sexual) and an individual may feel better contacting one of these. But there is an organisation for every possibility. All of these agencies are good.

What happens next depends upon who she might choose to contact, and what support they can offer. If Loren* decided to talk to her doctor, he might well refer her to services that would help her to overcome her terrors.

Like many victims, Loren* felt sure that no one would be able to help her. But when she was given the address and contact details, Loren* found (as many do) that she could not act upon this information immediately. She did not have the nerve. Things got worse before they got better. When the day came that she could no longer cope, she was amazed at the support and the listening that were available to her.

Chapter 4 – Scenario

When domestic violence shows effects on the children, the problems are immense. There is no way that problems with children (bed-wetting, self-harm, difficult behaviour) can be dealt with alone. The trouble here is that many an abused parent (whose self-belief is already at sub-zero) is going to feel they have failed in some way. The fear that social services will remove the child is very real and may lead to lies and cover-ups, as the parent tries to work things out.

But asking for help is not a sign of failure. It is the sensible and responsible thing to do. Admitting that there is a problem is always the first step and, once the right people understand that there is a problem, and that a parent is willing to accept help, help will be provided. Support will be developed for the parent as well as for the children.

Problems with children can provide the 'wake-up call' that is sometimes needed, to decide that there is a better way of life that it is worth working towards and fighting for. When the children begin to be visibly damaged by the bad situation, it is time to approach teachers and doctors to find out what sort of support is available. (Cook et al 2005)

Chapter 5 – Exercise

This is an exercise that asks you to describe yourself, as broadly as possible. It is often easiest to list the bad points and the things that seem to be failures, mistakes, or poor decisions. While it is important to list these negative items honestly, it is also important to list good things about yourself. This may include something that you did, once, in the past. Or it may include something that you hope to do in the future, because dreams and aspirations are still very important parts of us, providing hope which helps to keep us going.

Remembering yourself before you came into the bad relationship is not always easy. It can seem so long ago. But it is worth trying to recall the person you used to be. She is still there inside, waiting to be nourished and to form the basis of the person you will be in the future.

When you draw the comparisons, you might want to add in the things that you have learned, about yourself and about human nature, as a result of your experiences.

Chapter 6 – Exercise

This exercise takes self-description a little further and asks you to do it in a creative way, by using colour and drawings. Have as much fun as possible with this, as the fun is an important way of releasing the good feelings about yourself.

A good variation on this exercise is to draw only with your non-dominant hand – that is, with your left hand if you are right-handed and vice versa. Of course this is harder to do but, in fact, it pays dividends for two reasons. Firstly, it is more fun and the results are more amusing. Secondly, using your non-dominant hand opens up the less used side of your brain. That is a sure way to break out of the traps that your mental processes are in.

Chapter 7 – Exercise

This exercise may need a larger piece of paper, once you get started. It is up to you how you divide your paper – as a divided circle or as columns. That does not matter. What matters is that you begin to see how the lists overlap and that one item might appear in more than one place.

The point of this exercise is to see that there are things you want and to begin to see how you can achieve them. It may be difficult at first, but persevere. This exercise is all about focusing on the positives available in life and helping you to discover ways forward.

Chapter 8 – Exercise

In this chapter we looked at how to practically manage an escape from your bad situation. This exercise allows you to look at what is absolutely essential in life and how those things can be kept. If you are still thinking about leaving, this is a good exercise to do, since it will help you to clarify what you absolutely need. If you are ready to make that move, it is important to have a checklist of the essentials ready, so that once you have left there is absolutely nothing you need to go back for, risking putting yourself in harm's way.

Help List

Bringing information together, this chapter includes brief details on organisations that can help and a description of how the law has changed and developed over the last century. This information is short, so that it is easy to see at a glance which service(s) might be of most use to you. All of them do valuable work, but tend to operate in slightly different ways. They are listed in alphabetical order – which is why Women's Aid, the excellent backbone of what we do to help each other, appears towards the end of the list.
After these, the laws that aim to help victims of violence have been listed, showing the progress we have made. Some of these will be known to you, but others may surprise. These are included so that readers can clearly see how many rights they have, and how these can be used.

Al Anon

www.al-anon.org.uk
Helpline: 020 7403 0888
For families and partners of anyone with a drink problem.
Site includes a guide to your nearest meeting.
Includes links to Alateen.

Alateen

Alateen is for teenage relatives and friends of alcoholics. Alateen is part of Al-Anon. (see above)

Alcoholics Anonymous

Helpline: 0845 769 7555
Email: help@alcoholics-anonymous.org.uk.
(Services are staffed by volunteer members of A.A. For more general queries about A.A. you can write to the General Service Office:
Alcoholics Anonymous, PO Box 1, 10 Toft Green, York YO1 7ND).
Tel. 01904 644026 (Office hours only).
Email: gso@alcoholics.

Broken Rainbow

for LGBT (Lesbian, gay, bisexual and transgender) victims of domestic abuse
www.broken-rainbow.org.uk
Helpline 0300 999 5428

Childline (c/o NSPCC)

http://www.childline.org.uk
Tel: 0800 1111

Citizens Advice Bureau

Free legal advice.
Local phone numbers in every area.
Community Legal Service.
Information about applying for legal funding; all solicitors listed hold the 'quality mark'.
Helpline on 0845 345 4 345 (Minicom 0845 609 6677) for advice about benefits, tax credits, housing, employment, education or debt problems.

Court Service Website

www.courtservice.gov.uk
Guidance regarding injunctions, etc.
Domestic Violence DIY Injunction Handbook. Produced by Rights of Women; see page 84.

Drinkaware

www.drinkaware.co.uk
Outlines all you need to know about effects of alcohol, and when it is becoming a problem.

Expect Respect Toolkit

Created by Women's Aid; aimed at (but not exclusively for) teachers from Reception to Year 13. Not available in print. Download for free from www.womensaid.org.uk/toolkit
(It is recommended that you download the introduction and whatever section you need.)

Families Anonymous

Website: http://www.famanon.org.uk to find local meetings, etc.
Tel: 0845 1200 660
Email: office@famanon.org.uk
For families of drug users. (NB. There is a charge for this.)

Frank

www.talktofrank.com
Telephone: 0800 7766 00
Text: 82111
Deals with drugs, concerns, and getting help.
Includes 'find help', 'worried about someone' 'under pressure' and 'A-Z of drugs'.

Gingerbread

Website: www.gingerbread.org.uk
Freephone: 0808 802 0925
Provides advice and practical support for single parents.

Men's Advice Line

www.mensadviceline.org.uk
Helpline 0808 801 0327
For all men in abusive relationships.

MIND

Website: http://www.mind.org.uk
Infoline: 0300 123 3393 (also textphone at this number)
Email: info@mind.org.uk
Aims to help people take control of their mental health.
MIND's Legal Advice Service
0300 466 6463 or legal@mind.org.uk.

National Centre for Domestic Violence (NCDV)

Website: http://www.ncdv.org.uk
Aims to help you obtain an injunction to prevent further abuse from your partner. Free of charge, and will refer you to an experienced solicitor who, if you are eligible, will arrange Community Legal Service funding, or will accept payments in stages if you have to pay your own fees.

NSPCC

http://www.nspcc.org.uk
Links to Childline (see page 82)

Rape Crisis

Offers a series of support centres for women and girls across the country.
Tel: (Freephone) 0808 802 9999 (12-2.30pm and 7-9.30pm)

Refuge

http://www.refuge.org.uk
Telephone: 08008 2000 247 (helpline) shared with Women's Aid.

Respect

www.respect.uk.net
Helpline: 0808 802 4040
For abusers who want to stop abusive behaviour. Directory of information; www.respect.uk.net/pages/directory.html.

Rights of Women

A free legal advice line for women by women; especially regarding injunctions.
Telephone: 020 7251 6577 (or 020 7490 2562 textphone).
Open Tuesdays, Wednesdays and Thursday 2–4pm and 7–9pm, Friday, 12–2pm.
Also a free sexual violence legal advice line for women by women:
Telephone: 020 7251 8887
Textphone: 020 7490 2562
Open Mondays 11am-1pm and Tuesdays 10am-12pm.

Samaritans

UK helpline: 08457 90 90 90.
Republic of Ireland helpline: 1850 60 90 90.
Email: jo@samaritans.org
Write to: Chris, FREEPOST RSRB-KKBY-CYJK, P.O. Box 9090, Stirling, FK8 2SA
24-hour source of support

Women's Aid

Websites: www.womensaid.org.uk and www.thehideout.org.uk (for children)
Telephone: 0808 2000 247 (helpline) shared with Refuge
Email: helpline@womensaid.org.uk
Women's Aid is the core service for women suffering from domestic violence. They provide over 500 local services, including refuges, drop-in centres, a quarterly magazine and a 24-hour free helpline.

Zena

info@zenafoundation.com
Committed to helping women fleeing from either culturally aggravated murder (CAM) or domestic violence (DV).

The Law

Details taken from Harwood S. 2011, and SAFE magazine, various issues 2010.

- 1923 – Matrimonial Causes Act made grounds or divorce the same for both men and women.
- 1937 – Matrimonial Causes Act extended – includes cruelty as grounds for divorce.
- 1965 – Race Relations Act (strengthened 1968 and 1975).
- 1967 – Abortion is decriminalised.
- 1967 – Family Planning Clinics available to all women, married and unmarried.
- 1971 – Refuge established http://www.refuge.org.uk.
- 1972 – First Women's Aid refuge set up in Chiswick.
- 1974 – National Women's Aid Federation established.
- 1975 – Sex Discrimination Act.
- 1976 – (First) Domestic Violence Act.
- 1977 – First Rape Crisis Centre opens (London).
- 1977 – Women and children legally recognised as homeless, if at risk from domestic violence.
- 1985 – Prohibition of Female Circumcision Act.
- 1994 – Rape in marriage becomes a crime.
- 1994 – United Nations Declaration on the elimination of Violence states that violence against women violates their human rights.
- 1996 – Family Law Act.
- 2003 – Female Genital Mutilation Act.
- 2004 – Forced Marriage Unit.

- 2004 – Domestic Violence, Crime and Victims Act (guidance can be downloaded from http://www.legislation.gov.uk/ukpga/2004/28/contents.
- 2005 – Civil Partnerships Act.
- 2007 – Sexual Violence and Abuse Action Plan (SVAAP).
- 2007 – Forced Marriage (Civil Protection) Act – protects against forced marriage.
- 2008 – The Crown Prosecution Service Violence Against Women (VAW) strategy and action plans.
- 2009 – Violence against Women and Girls Strategy.
- 2010 – Equality Act (implemented April 2011).
- 2010 – National Union of Students survey ('Hidden Marks'); a study of women students' experiences of harassment, stalking and sexual assault'. Available from http://www.nus.org.uk/en/News/News/Hidden-Marks.
- 2010 – Ministry of Justice announces 14 new domestic violence courts in England and Wales.
- 2011 – End violence against women coalition statement. www.endviolenceagainstwomen.org.uk.

2011 – Clare's Law (ongoing).

Clare's Law

At the end of July 2011, a campaign known as 'Clare's Law' was launched. (It was modelled on 'Sarah's Law', which gives parents the right to check on paedophiles in their area, after the murder of schoolgirl Sarah Payne.) Clare's Law is named after Clare Wood, who was killed by man she met on Facebook. In the proposed legislation, women who use the Internet to find boyfriends win the right to force the police to reveal if their partner has a history of violence. Whether this would actually help is a matter of discussion.

A relationship that becomes violent may not necessarily have any antecedents. Violence develops, and while there is no doubt that once the line has been crossed, things (and people) are never going to be the same again, on the day before we would not necessarily know that someone was likely to become violent. He may never have crossed that line before, or it may not be on record. 'He has a temper' is a good warning sign. This is probably someone we should avoid, because the chances are that one day we will become its focus. Potential for violence is something that we spot by interacting with a person. Checking his history suggests that we are already worried, and it may be that we have 'gut feelings' about him, however charming. Gut feelings are ignored at our peril.

Libby Brooks says, 'If a woman is warned, but the relationship is in its early stages and she convinces herself that things will be different this time, how much more vicious will the national sport of victim-blaming be when she finally reports an assault? Worse, what happens when she confronts her new boyfriend with the information she has received?' (Libby Brooks, The Guardian, 21 July 2011)

Because violence is not a simple thing, exactly how Clare's Law would protect those most at risk is not clear. Wary women would still listen to their feelings about someone, and stay away from risk. More trusting women would still find themselves slipping into a dangerous place, before thinking to check out their partner's history – if he has one. By the time violence has reared its head; most victims might find that they are in just as deep with it as without it. And the existence of Clare's Law might also work against women in court, who could then be described as having ignored knowledge when it was available. The reality of course is that we all make character judgements (some good, some bad) and then get on with life. We make mistakes. It has taken victims of violence many years to get fair hearings in court, but it is possible here to open a door which allows acquittal on points of law.

'"He has a temper" is a good warning sign.'

All relationships are a gamble, not just those formed online, but also those begun via services such as online dating (now very big business!) and in the normal ways. The best way forward is to be wary, and not to rely upon 'records', which may or may not accurately describe the man as he is now. When domestic violence destroys a person's self-confidence and esteem, the last thing they want is to be further demolished by a clever lawyer for the defence. That would not be justice.

However, if an assault takes place, the existence of Clare's Law gives all the more reason to report it to the police, and to document it properly.

Finally . . .

While it is not possible to cover every situation in any book, our stories have more than enough common threads, so that we can learn from each other – and learn how to support each other. In domestic violence, age and income do not matter. Anyone can be at risk. Victims of violence may be male as well as female, gay or heterosexual.

What matters is that we discover the way out of the trap; back to the good person we were always meant to be.

You are a survivor.

Glossary

Acute
Abrupt onset. Acute, also an illness that is of short duration, rapidly progresses, and is in need of urgent care.

Acute stress disorder
The anxiety and behavioural disturbances that develop within a month of exposure to extreme trauma. These usually begin during or shortly following the trauma.

Addiction
A long-term relapsing condition characterised by abuse of drugs or alcohol, and by long-lasting chemical changes in the brain. Stopping is very difficult and causes severe physical and mental reactions from withdrawal. The genetic factors predisposing to addiction exist, but are not yet fully understood.

ADHD
Attention deficit hyperactivity disorder has symptoms that may begin in childhood and continue into adulthood. Sufferers have difficulty sustaining attention to one task at a time.

Agoraphobia
Mostly thought to be a fear of public places, it is now believed that agoraphobia develops as a complication of panic attacks.

Anhedonia
Loss of the capacity to experience pleasure. The inability to gain pleasure from normally pleasurable experiences. A core clinical feature of depression, schizophrenia, and some other mental illnesses.

Antidepressant
Any drug, used to prevent or treat depression.

Anxiety
A feeling of apprehension and fear characterised by physical symptoms such as palpitations, sweating, and feelings of stress.

Anxiety disorder
Anxiety disorders are serious medical illnesses. These disorders fill people's lives with overwhelming anxiety and fear. Unlike the relatively mild, brief anxiety caused by a stressful event, anxiety disorders are chronic, relentless, and can grow progressively worse if not treated.

Behavioural control
Lack of control. Problems with aggression, impulse control and sleep problems.

Bipolar disorder
A mood disorder sometimes called manic-depressive illness or manic-depression that involves cycles of depression and elation or mania. Both the depressive and manic cycles may be severe and often lead to impaired functioning.

Borderline personality disorder
A serious mental illness with pervasive instability in moods, interpersonal relationships, self-image, and behaviour. This instability often disrupts family and work life, long-term planning, and the individual's sense of self-identity.

Chronic
Lasting a long time.

Cognitive
The process of being aware, knowing, thinking, learning and judging.

Cognitive therapy
A relatively short-term form of psychotherapy based on the concept that the way we think about things affects how we feel emotionally. Cognitive therapy focuses on present thinking, behaviour and communication, rather than on past experiences and is oriented towards problem solving. Cognitive therapy has been applied to a broad range of problems including depression, anxiety, panic, fears, eating disorders, substance abuse, and personality problems.

Craving
A strong need, perhaps to drink or use drugs.

Depersonalisation
Sufferers say that they feel 'detached from their body'.

Depression
An illness that involves the body, mood, and thoughts, which affects the way a person eats and sleeps, the way one feels about oneself, and the way one thinks about things. A depressive disorder is not the same as a passing sad mood. It is not a sign of personal weakness or a condition that can be wished away. People with a depressive disease cannot merely 'pull themselves together' and get better. Without treatment, symptoms can last for weeks, months, or years. Appropriate treatment, however, can help most people with depression.

Diagnosis
The nature of a disease; the identification of an illness.

Dissociation
A perceived detachment of the mind from the emotional state or even from the body. Dissociation is characterised by a sense of the world as a dreamlike or unreal place and may be accompanied by poor memory of the specific events, which in severe form is known as 'dissociative amnesia'.

Fatigue
Feeling tired. A lessened capacity for work and reduced efficiency of accomplishment, usually accompanied by a feeling of weariness and tiredness. Fatigue can be acute and come on suddenly, or chronic and persistant.

Generalised anxiety disorder (GAD)
A condition characterised by 6 months or more of chronic, exaggerated worry and tension that is unfounded or much more severe than the normal anxiety most people experience. People with GAD usually expect the worst.

Hyperactivity
A higher than normal level of activity. An organ can be described as hyperactive if it is more active than usual. Behaviour can also be hyperactive.

Hyperarousal
A specific cluster of PTSD symptoms. This cluster includes symptoms that stem from experiencing high levels of anxiety. Being 'jumpy' or easily startled.

Imagery
Both a mental process (as in imagining) and a wide variety of procedures used in therapy to encourage changes in attitudes, behaviour, or physiological reactions.

Impulsivity
Inclined to act on impulse rather than thought. People who are overly impulsive, seem unable to curb their immediate reactions or think before they act. As a result, they may blurt out answers to questions or inappropriate comments, or run into the street without looking. Their impulsivity may make it hard for a child to wait for things they want or to take their turn in games. They may grab a toy from another child or hit when they are upset.

Injury
Harm or hurt. The injury may be accidental or deliberate.

Learning disability
A disorder beginning in childhood characterised by difficulty with certain skills such as reading or writing in individuals with normal intelligence. Learning disorders affect the ability to interpret what one sees and hears or the ability to link information from different parts of the brain. These limitations can show up in many ways: as specific difficulties with spoken and written language, coordination, self-control, or attention. Such difficulties extend to schoolwork and can impede learning to read or write, or to do maths.

Loss of control
E.g. in alcoholism, not being able to stop drinking once drinking has begun.

Manic
Refers to a mood disorder in which a person seems 'high', euphoric, expansive, sometimes agitated, hyper-excitable, with 'flights' of ideas and speech.

OCD
Obsessive-compulsive disorder.

Panic
A sudden strong feeling of fear that prevents reasonable thought or action.

Personality disorder
A long-standing disorder characterised by the chronic use of mechanisms of coping in an inappropriate manner. Personality disorders are enduring and persistent styles of behaviour and thought. Personality disorders encompass a group of behavioural disorders that are different and distinct from the psychotic and neurotic disorders. Defined as 'an enduring pattern of inner experience and

behaviour that differs markedly from the expectations of the individual's culture, is pervasive and inflexible, has an onset in adolescence or early adulthood, is stable over time, and leads to distress or impairment'. (DSM 1V).

Phobia
An unreasonable sort of fear that can cause avoidance and panic. Phobias are a relatively common type of anxiety disorder.

Physical dependence
Withdrawal symptoms occur after stopping drinking or using drugs. These symptoms include nausea, shakiness, anxiety and sweating. Finally, hallucinations may occur.

Prevalence
The proportion of individuals in a population having a disease. A statistical concept referring to the number of cases of a disease that are present in a particular population at a given time.

Psychotherapy
The treatment of a behaviour disorder, mental illness, or any other condition by psychological means. Psychotherapy may use insight, persuasion, suggestion, reassurance, and instruction so that patients may see themselves and their problems more realistically and wish to cope effectively with them.

PTSD
Post-traumatic stress disorder.

Rape
Forced sexual intercourse; sexual assault; sexual intercourse between an adult and a minor.

Recurrent
'Back again'. Returns after an intermission.

Regress
To return or go back to a pattern of behaviour characteristic of a younger age. In reference to disease, to 'regress' means tending to worsen.

Relapse
The return of signs and symptoms of a disease after a patient has enjoyed a remission.

Remission
Freedom from symptoms.

Schizophrenia
One of several brain diseases whose symptoms may include loss of personality (flat affect), agitation, catatonia, confusion, psychosis, unusual behaviour, and withdrawal.

Shock
A critical condition brought on by a sudden drop in blood flow through the body. The circulatory system fails to maintain adequate blood flow. The signs and symptoms of shock include low blood pressure (hypotension), overbreathing (hyperventilation); a weak rapid pulse; cold clammy greyish-bluish (cyanotic) skin; decreased urine flow (oliguria); and mental changes (a sense of great anxiety and foreboding, confusion and, sometimes, combativeness).

Signs and symptoms
Any subjective evidence of disease. Pain, anxiety and fatigue are all symptoms. They are sensations only the patient can perceive. In contrast, a sign is objective evidence of disease. A bloody nose is a sign. It is evident to the patient, doctor, nurse and other observers.

Social anxiety disorder
Excessive fear of embarrassment in social situations that is extremely intrusive and can have debilitating effects on personal and professional relationships. Also called social phobia.

Somatisation
The process by which psychological distress is expressed as physical symptoms. This is an unconscious process.

Stress
Forces from the outside world impinging on the individual. Stress is a normal part of life that can help us learn and grow. Conversely, excess stress can cause us significant problems.

Substance abuse
The excessive use of a substance, especially alcohol or a drug. (There is no universally accepted definition of substance abuse.)

Suicidal
Relates to the taking of one's own life. A suicidal gesture, suicidal thought, or suicidal act may not be successful, but the intention is serious.

Symbiosis
Symbiotic relationships (among plants and animals) include those in which one organism lives on another or where one partner lives inside the other. In some symbiotic relationships, both symbionts entirely depend on each other for survival. Others can but do not have to live with the other organism. In humans the symbiotic relationship describes a very close and usually unhealthy interdependence.

Syndrome
A collection of signs and symptoms that tend to occur together and reflect the presence of a particular disease or an increased chance of developing it.

Therapy
The treatment of disease.

Tolerance
In alcoholism or drug abuse, the need to drink greater amounts of alcohol, or use increasing amounts of drugs.

Torture
An act by which severe pain or suffering, whether physical or mental, is intentionally inflicted on a person. Survivors of torture often suffer from physical and psychological symptoms and disabilities. Torture may result in psychological symptoms of depression (most common), post-traumatic stress disorder, marked sleep disturbances and alterations in self-perceptions together with feelings of powerlessness, fear, guilt and shame.

Trauma
Any injury, whether physically or emotionally inflicted. Trauma has both a medical and a psychiatric definition. Medically – a serious or critical bodily injury, wound, or shock. In psychiatry – refers to an experience that is emotionally painful, distressful, or shocking, which often results in lasting mental and physical effects.

Withdrawal symptoms
Abnormal physical or psychological features that follow the abrupt discontinuation of a drug that has the capability of producing physical dependence. Common withdrawal symptoms include sweating, insomnia, vomiting, tremor, and anxiety.

References

Abrahams, Hilary
Re-building Lives after Domestic Violence
Pub. Jessica Kingsley, 2010

Lundy Bancroft
Why Does He Do That? Inside the Minds of Angry and Controlling Men
Berkley Publishing Group 2003

Bradbury-Jones et al
Improving the health care of women living with domestic abuse
Nursing Standard, vol 25, no. 43, June 2011

Butler, Eleri
Standing up against violence against women
Safe Magazine, issue 33, Spring 2010

Eve S. Buzawa, Carl G. Buzawa and Evan Stark
Responding to Domestic Violence: The Integration of Criminal Justice and Human Services
Sage Publications, Inc. 2011

Cook, A., Spinazzola, J., Ford, J., Lanktree, C., et al.
(2005) Complex trauma in children and adolescents. Psychiatric Annals, 35:5, 390-398.

Courtois CA, Ford JD (eds)
Treating Complex Traumatic Stress Disorders – an evidence-based guide
The Guilford Press 2009

Foa, Edna B., Terence M. Keane, Matthew J. Friedman and Judith A. Cohen
Effective Treatments for PTSD: Practice Guidelines from the International Society for Traumatic Stress Studies
Guildford Press 2009

Griffiths S, et al
Benefits of identifying need as well as risk for victims/survivors of domestic violence
Safe Magazine issue 37, Spring 2011

Sam Harrington-Lowe
Alcoholism: The Family Guide
Need2Know 2008

Harwood S.
Celebrating 100 years of International Women's Day
Safe magazine, issue 37, spring 2011

Judith Lewis Herman
Trauma and Recovery: The Aftermath of Violence – from Domestic Abuse to Political Terror
Basic Books 1997

Humphreys K, Gorard L
Changing Young Hearts and Minds; Women's Aid Expect Respect Tookit
Safe Magazine, issue 33, Spring 2009

Catherine Itzin, Ann Taket and Sarah Barter-Godfrey
Domestic and Sexual Violence and Abuse: Tackling the Health and Mental Health Effects
Routledge 2010

Kate Iwi and Chris Newman
Picking up the Pieces After Domestic Violence: A Practical Resource for Supporting Parenting Skills
Jessica Kingsley Publishers 2011

Eva Leveton
Healing Collective Trauma Using Sociodrama and Drama Therapy
Springer Publishing Company LLC 2010

David Mann and Valerie Cunningham
The Past in the Present
Routledge 2009

McGarry, J, Simpson C,
The impact of domestic abuse on the lives and health of older women.
Safe Magazine, issue 35, Autumn 2010

National Institute of Mental Health
Post-Traumatic Stress Disorder (PTSD)
Kindle Edition – 2011

Neale J, Worrell M
Visibility, responsibility and identity in domestic murder-suicide
Safe Magazine, issue 33, Spring 2010

Jim O'Shea
Abuse: Domestic Violence, Workplace and School Bullying
Cork University Press 2011

Tevillion K et al
Domestic Violence; responding to the needs of patients
Nursing Standard, vol 25, no 26, March 2011

Watson J
Crown Prosecution Service Violence against Women strategy and action
Safe Magazine, issue 33, Spring 2009

Bibliography

Mario R. Dewalt
Domestic Violence: Law Enforcement Response and Legal Perspectives
(Criminal Justice, Law Enforcement and Corrections) Nova Science Publishers Inc 2011

Melissa J. Doak
Child Abuse and Domestic Violence
(Information Plus Reference: Child Abuse & Domestic Violence)
Cengage Gale 2011

Kevin A. Fall and Shareen Howard
Alternatives to Domestic Violence: A Homework Manual for Battering Intervention Groups
Routledge 2011

Featherstone L
We want to make a difference
Safe Magazine issue 36, Winter 2011

Louise Gerdes
Domestic Violence (Opposing Viewpoints)
Greenhaven Press 2011

Nicola Groves and Terry Thomas
Domestic Violence and Criminal Justice
Willan 2011

Peter G. Jaffe, David A. Wolfe and Marcie Campbell
Growing Up with Domestic Violence (Advances in Psychotherapy: Evidence-Based Practice)
Hogrefe Publishing 2011

Thomas B. James
Domestic Violence: The 12 Things You Aren't Supposed to Know
Aventine Press 2003

Schechter DS, Coates, SW, Kaminer T, Coots T, Zeanah CH, Davies M, Schonfield IS, Marshall RD, Liebowitz MR Trabka KA, McCaw J, Myers MM (2008).
Distorted maternal mental representations and atypical behavior in a clinical sample of violence-exposed mothers and their toddlers. Journal of Trauma and Dissociation, 9(2), 123-149.

Schechter DS, Willheim E (2009).
Disturbances of attachment and parental psychopathology in early childhood. Infant and Early Childhood Mental Health Issue. Child and Adolescent Psychiatry Clinics of North America, 18(3), 665-687.

Mary Lay Schuster and Amy D. Propen
Victim Advocacy in the Courtroom: Persuasive Practices in Domestic Violence and Child Protection Cases (Northeastern Series on Gender, Crime, and Law) Northeastern University Press 2011

Sandra M. Stith, Eric E. McCollum and Karen H. Rosen
Couples Therapy for Domestic Violence: Finding Safe Solutions
American Psychological Association (APA) 2011

Taylor, S
Putting Survivors back at the heart of the violence against women and girls movement
Safe Magazine issue 36, Winter 2011

Wener C
Communicating the message; the value of working together
Safe Magazine, issue 35, Autumn 2010

Need – 2 – Know

Need - 2 - Know

Available Titles Include ...

Allergies A Parent's Guide
ISBN 978-1-86144-064-8 £8.99

Autism A Parent's Guide
ISBN 978-1-86144-069-3 £8.99

Blood Pressure The Essential Guide
ISBN 978-1-86144-067-9 £8.99

Dyslexia and Other Learning Difficulties
A Parent's Guide ISBN 978-1-86144-042-6 £8.99

Bullying A Parent's Guide
ISBN 978-1-86144-044-0 £8.99

Epilepsy The Essential Guide
ISBN 978-1-86144-063-1 £8.99

Your First Pregnancy The Essential Guide
ISBN 978-1-86144-066-2 £8.99

Gap Years The Essential Guide
ISBN 978-1-86144-079-2 £8.99

Secondary School A Parent's Guide
ISBN 978-1-86144-093-8 £9.99

Primary School A Parent's Guide
ISBN 978-1-86144-088-4 £9.99

Applying to University The Essential Guide
ISBN 978-1-86144-052-5 £8.99

ADHD The Essential Guide
ISBN 978-1-86144-060-0 £8.99

Student Cookbook – Healthy Eating The Essential Gui
ISBN 978-1-86144-069-3 £8.99

Multiple Sclerosis The Essential Guide
ISBN 978-1-86144-086-0 £8.99

Coeliac Disease The Essential Guide
ISBN 978-1-86144-087-7 £9.99

Special Educational Needs A Parent's Guide
ISBN 978-1-86144-116-4 £9.99

The Pill An Essential Guide
ISBN 978-1-86144-058-7 £8.99

University A Survival Guide
ISBN 978-1-86144-072-3 £8.99

View the full range at **www.need2knowbooks.co.uk**. To order our titles call **01733 898103**, email **sales@n2kbooks.com** or visit the website. Selected ebooks available online.

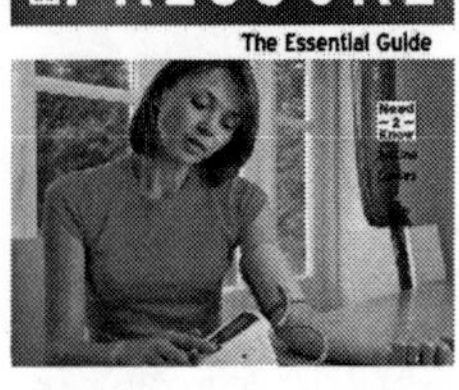

CARDIFF COLLEGE LRC
32302
44882

Need - 2 - Know, Remus House, Coltsfoot Drive, Peterborough, PE2 9BF